Modern Web Apps using Rust

Build full-stack applications using Rust-based Leptos framework, GraphQL, WebAssembly, and cloud-native deployment

Nira Talvyn

Published by: GitforGits

Publisher: Sonal Dhandre

www.gitforgits.com

support@gitforgits.com

Printed in India

First Printing: January 2025

ISBN: 978-93-49174-87-0

Cover Design by: Kitten Publishing

Prologue

We are on the cusp of a new era in web development, where Rust's performance and safety are set to transform the way we build interactive, scalable applications. Just imagine the possibilities of shipping code that runs at near-native speed in the browser, while sharing the same language, types, and crates between client and server! Picture microservices that never block, servers that self-heal under load, and real-time features that flow seamlessly from backend to UI. That future is here, and it begins with this book!

From the very first moment I discovered the incredible potential of Rust for web apps, I saw so much more than just a fast systems language. I saw an incredible unified toolchain that can compile both network services and front-end logic into WebAssembly. I saw Leptos enabling reactive components without a JavaScript runtime, sharing Serde models across every layer. I saw an incredible architecture where inventory, orders, and user accounts live in distinct modules, yet integrate so smoothly that shipping a change feels effortless. I saw the most amazing real-time WebSocket updates driving stock levels and order statuses, incredible end-to-end tests catching regressions before they reach production, and GitHub Actions flipping the switch from code commit to global rollout with no human clicks.

In the chapters ahead, you and I will build LibroCommerce, a sample book-selling application that evolves as you progress. You'll start by setting up Rust, Cargo, and Leptos in VS Code, compiling your first WebAssembly bundle, and watching "Hello, LibroCommerce!" light up your browser. You'll design a microservice-inspired architecture, splitting functionality into inventory, orders, and accounts, then connect those modules with Axum handlers and SQLx queries. You'll model data with Serde-annotated structs, implement CRUD operations, and secure every endpoint with JWT, OAuth2, and Argon2-hashed passwords.

Then, we'll add real-time magic—broadcast channels in Tokio, WebSocket endpoints in Axum, and reactive signals in Leptos—so your UI updates instantly when stock changes or an order moves from pending to shipped. You'll get to write Playwright end-to-end tests that spin up headless browsers, place orders, and assert live status updates, all inside your continuous integration pipeline. You'll be thrilled to package each service and the frontend into Docker containers, deploy to Kubernetes with zero-downtime rollouts, and watch as your cluster scales under load. And that's not all — you'll dive into the world of serverless and edge computing, mastering the art of running Rust functions in AWS Lambda and Leptos SSR at Cloudflare Workers. Get ready to take your app to new heights, reaching users worldwide in the blink of an eye!

This book is so much more than a mere collection of examples—it's an exhilarating hands-on journey! You'll get to write over a hundred code snippets, inspect them in VS Code, and see immediate feedback in browser and terminal. You will troubleshoot errors, refine performance with tuned Tokio threads and SQLx pools, and emerge with confidence in building production-grade web apps in Rust. By the time you reach the end, you will have taken that bold first step—

from curiosity to creation—and you will be armed with patterns, practices, and working solutions that will let you continue innovating long after you turn the final page. Welcome to "Modern Web Apps using Rust."

Let's dive in!

Content

Preface

In this book, you'll dive into the world of web development with Rust and Leptos. First, you install a solid Rust toolchain and set up Leptos in VS Code, and then you see your first "Hello World" interface rendered via WebAssembly right away. So, first you'll design a microservice-inspired book-selling sample app, called LibroCommerce, into inventory, orders, and user accounts. Then, you'll connect each piece with Axum handlers, SQLx queries, and shared Serde models.

By the time you get to Chapter 3, you'll have built a nonblocking, Tokio-driven server that handles dynamic routes, powers Leptos SSR pages, and secures endpoints with JWT and OAuth2. Then, you add real-time features: WebSockets send stock updates and order-status events to reactive Leptos signals, keeping the UI and backend in sync. As you go, you'll be writing end-to-end Playwright tests and setting up GitHub Actions so that every commit runs Rust tests, Playwright scenarios, Docker builds, and Kubernetes rollouts automatically. You'll learn how to connect to PostgreSQL with an async pool, model Books, Users, and Orders with Serde-annotated Rust structs, and implement CRUD, password hashing with Argon2, encrypted backups, and session stores in Redis. Performance tuning shows you how to optimize Tokio threads, tune SQLx pools, stream large result sets, debounce client inputs, and apply backpressure. At last, you put each microservice and frontend into Docker containers, deploy them with Kubernetes, and then use serverless and edge computing. That means running order logic as AWS Lambda functions and serving SSR pages from Cloudflare Workers. This way, you can cut down on latency for users worldwide.

It's packed with over 100 bite-sized examples and ready-to-run solutions, and it'll walk you through building and operating a production-style web application in Rust, step-by-step. You won't become a Rust language expert, but you'll finish ready to design, code, test, and deploy modern web apps.

In this book you will learn how to:

- Start using Rust and Leptos with VS Code to develop web applications using WebAssembly.
- Architect microservices with inventory, orders, and user modules for modular, scalable applications.
- Make servers that respond to user activity and are not blocked by other users. Use Tokio and Axum with dynamic routing and concurrency.
- Employ business logic with SQLX, transactions, and external API integration for real-world workflows.

- Protect your devices with JWT, OAuth2, Argon2 password hashing, HttpOnly cookies, and TLS encryption.
- Handle database state asynchronously, define Serde data models, and perform efficient CRUD operations.
- Utilize WebSockets, Leptos signals, and broadcast channels to enable real-time updates.
- Perform end-to-end testing with Playwright, integration tests, and automated CI pipelines for reliability.
- Put microservices and the frontend into containers using Docker, and use Kubernetes to orchestrate them so they can be deployed without any downtime.
- Take advantage of serverless functions and edge computing to reduce latency and expand globally as needed.

GitforGits

Prerequisites

This book is for web developers, rust programmers, app developers, backend developers whi are willing to explore, practice and introduce the power of Rust into their web apps. Prior knowledge of rust coding would be helpful.

Codes Usage

Are you in need of some helpful code examples to assist you in our programming and documentation? Look no further! Our book offers a wealth of supplemental material, including code examples and exercises.

Not only is this book here to aid you in getting our job done, but you have our permission to use the example code in our programs and documentation. However, please note that if you are reproducing a significant portion of the code, we do require you to contact us for permission.

But don't worry, using several chunks of code from this book in our program or answering a question by citing our book and quoting example code does not require permission. But if you do choose to give credit, an attribution typically includes the title, author, publisher, and ISBN. For example, "Modern Web Apps using Rust by Nira Talvyn".

If you are unsure whether our intended use of the code examples falls under fair use or the permissions outlined above, please do not hesitate to reach out to us at support@gitforgits.com.

We are happy to assist and clarify any concerns.

Acknowledgement

I owe a tremendous debt of gratitude to GitforGits, for their unflagging enthusiasm and wise counsel throughout the entire process of writing this book. Their knowledge and careful editing helped make sure the piece was useful for people of all reading levels and comprehension skills. In addition, I'd like to thank everyone involved in the publishing process for their efforts in making this book a reality. Their efforts, from copyediting to advertising, made the project what it is today.

Finally, I'd like to express my gratitude to everyone who has shown me unconditional love and encouragement throughout my life. Their support was crucial to the completion of this book. I appreciate our help with this endeavour and our continued interest in my career.

CHAPTER 1: SETTING UP RUST & LEPTOS ENVIRONMENT

Overview

In this chapter, we will start an exciting journey that gets the ball rolling on building LibroCommerce, our interactive book selling platform using Rust and Leptos. We will learn to install and configure Rust via Cargo on a Linux system and set up our development environment using VS Code with essential extensions. We will set up a Git repository, create a GitHub repository, and use effective branching strategies to manage our project efficiently.

Next, we will design a modular folder structure that separates server, client, and common code, making development and maintenance easier. Finally, we will create and run a simple "Hello World" interface using Leptos to show basic client-server communication and start building a fully interactive web app. This chapter's got everything you need to get up to speed fast. We will get to put our knowledge into practice and learn the ropes. This will give you a leg up on the rest of the advanced stuff we'll cover later.

Why Rust & Leptos for Web Apps?

It's an exciting time to start working in web application development, but it can also be a bit challenging. In this topic, we will learn how Rust, which is usually associated with systems programming, has made its way into the world of web apps. We will also see how its partnership with Leptos has led to the creation of a strong tech stack for developing responsive, secure, and high-performance applications. As you go through this stuff, we will learn about the pros of Rust when it comes to runtime performance and memory safety. We will also see how Leptos uses these strengths to deliver a modern web framework. We'll go over every detail with you in a way that's fun and interactive. We will learn the concepts and feel confident using them on our own projects.

Rust's Emergence in Web

Over the past few years, Rust has made a huge splash in the world of web application development, and you're now seeing it gain popularity in areas where speed, efficiency, and safety are super important. Developers usually used languages like JavaScript, Python, or Java to create web applications, but Rust has changed all that. It's all about performance and reliability now. We will see that the language, which is mostly known for system-level programming, has evolved through community-driven innovations and a robust ecosystem. These days, a lot of people are using Rust to build full-stack applications, and its growing list of web development libraries and frameworks shows just how flexible it is. With developers all over the world pitching in, the language has reached a level of maturity that makes it a great choice for scalable web solutions. This change shows that people are putting a lot more importance on making the most of resources and making sure things are very safe.

Engine behind Modern Web Apps

Recently, I've been using Rust a lot, and I have to say, it's pretty amazing. It's got a level of performance that's hard to match with other languages. Rust compiles straight into machine code, so our web application runs closer to the hardware without the overhead that traditional garbage-collected languages introduce. This compile-time optimization leads to lower latency and better throughput, features that become more important as our application scales to handle more users and data. The language's strict compiler checks, which enforce type and concurrency safety, help you avoid a lot of common mistakes in systems programming. When you build LibroCommerce, for example, we will see how this performance boost lets the platform handle a lot of transactions quickly and with almost no delay. This capability directly translates to an enhanced user experience where every search, page load, and transaction occurs swiftly, contributing to a more responsive platform overall.

One of the things that makes Rust stand out is its strong emphasis on memory safety. We will get safeguards at compile time that prevent issues like data races and segmentation faults, which have traditionally led to critical vulnerabilities in many applications. Rust makes it so that our code is less likely to have those pesky bugs that can cause security holes or system crashes by having strict rules on ownership, borrowing, and lifetimes. For web apps, where user data integrity and security are a top priority, these safety features give you the confidence to handle sensitive tasks without sacrificing performance. As you build LibroCommerce, we will see how Rust's safety constructs help you develop backend services that are solid even under heavy load. This means fewer runtime errors and a more secure experience for our users, plus lower maintenance costs over time. Rust's memory model makes sure our web app stays top-notch and secure from start to finish.

Introducing Leptos

So, you're getting into the world of interactive web development, right? Well, we will probably run into Leptos pretty soon. It's a lightweight, reactive framework that's designed to work with Rust. Leptos brings the power of Rust to frontend development through WebAssembly, enabling you to write highly interactive user interfaces that run natively in modern browsers. The framework has a component-based architecture, which makes it easy for you to build reusable, modular UI elements that adapt to dynamic data changes. When you add Leptos to our project, you're not just using a new tool — you're adopting a whole new way of thinking where you have control of both client-side and server-side logic with a single language and toolset. This integration lets you develop apps that are not only fast but also handle complex interactions in real time, making sure the overall user experience stays smooth and consistent. Leptos has a modern web app with a forward-thinking design that anticipates the needs of users who demand responsiveness and elegance in every interaction.

When you put the strength of Rust together with the flexibility and quickness of Leptos, you get a tech stack that's solid in how well it works and how well it performs. In a world where web apps are expected to be secure, easy to maintain, and fast, this pairing offers you the best of both worlds. Leptos uses Rust's awesome asynchronous features, thanks to runtimes like Tokio, to handle concurrent operations without sacrificing performance. The end result is a stack where the frontend and backend communicate seamlessly, sharing robust libraries and idiomatic Rust code across the entire project. For example, in LibroCommerce, we will see how state management and live data updates are handled with precision, thanks to the smooth integration of Leptos with Rust's type-safe and efficient concurrency model. As you keep working on our development journey, we will see how the combination makes debugging easier and boosts productivity, encouraging a more iterative, test-driven approach to building scalable web applications.

In addition to technical strengths, adopting Rust and Leptos empowers you to take full control over both client and server aspects of web development using a consistent programming model. This consistency not only minimizes the learning curve but also streamlines collaborative work, especially when managing projects through platforms like GitHub. With VS Code as our chosen IDE, you will experience a seamless development environment that brings together intelligent code completion, static analysis, and integrated debugging. As you develop LibroCommerce, you will learn to orchestrate various components—ranging from dynamic APIs to real-time user interfaces—all written in Rust and compiled into efficient WebAssembly modules through Leptos. This consistent approach simplifies version control and continuous integration, as every change is tracked and refined using GitHub Actions. Ultimately, this stack empowers you to create applications that meet modern performance expectations while ensuring that our codebase remains resilient, secure, and easy to maintain.

Future of Web Development

As you get ready to build LibroCommerce and move forward into web application development, the Rust and Leptos stack is a top choice that meets the needs of modern users. We will get unparalleled performance and memory safety from Rust, and the transformative capabilities of Leptos, which let you craft interactive, resilient, and aesthetically pleasing user interfaces. This blend makes sure our apps can handle a lot of users at once, give you updates in real-time, and keep our users' data safe, all while keeping things simple and working smoothly. As you go through this process, we will see that every part—from the low-level performance improvements to the high-level interactive designs—is created to help you quickly turn ideas into working, industry-ready web applications.

In this chapter, you've seen how Rust's entry into web app development marks a big shift towards secure and efficient programming. You've also seen how Leptos enhances this potential by bridging the gap between powerful backend performance and dynamic frontend interactivity. We've set the stage for why teaming up with Rust and Leptos is a smart move, both practically and creatively. It's an awesome chance to dive into fresh web development approaches. As you move forward, we will keep using these strengths to build LibroCommerce bit by bit, turning theoretical ideas into real-world features that you can see and tweak in an interactive setting.

If you go with this stack, we will be on the cutting edge of web development and ready for a future where performance, safety, and user experience go hand in hand. With each lesson, we will learn techniques that'll give you the skills to build solid applications for a digital landscape that's always changing.

Installing IDE, Libraries & Other Tools

To begin with, we roll up our sleeves and get you set up with everything you need to start building LibroCommerce on our Linux system. We'll install Rust using Cargo, configure VS Code along with the Rust Analyzer extension, and fetch key crates that will power our project. As you follow along, we will see that LibroCommerce is our practical, live example, which is a modern book selling platform that tries to simulate the real-world application of Rust and Leptos.

Installing Rust

When you decide to build high-performance web applications using Rust, the first step is installing the language itself, and Cargo, the built-in package manager and build system. We'll use the official Rust installer, rustup, to set everything up.

On our terminal, you can download and run rustup with the following command:

```
curl --proto '=https' --tlsv1.2 -sSf https://sh.rustup.rs | sh
```

This command downloads rustup and installs the latest stable version of Rust, setting up Cargo along the way. Cargo is our trusty tool for handling dependencies, building projects, and running tests, which means every time you work on LibroCommerce, you are working with a streamlined and efficient toolchain. As Cargo fetches and compiles libraries, it ensures that our development process remains manageable, efficient, and reliable. Once rustup is installed, you can verify the installation by running **`rustc --version`** and **`cargo --version`**. With these commands, you can see which versions of the tools you're working with, and we will be ready to move onto the next stage of our setup.

Configuring VS Code & Crates

VS Code is our chosen IDE because of its flexibility, rich ecosystem of extensions, and its seamless integration with Linux. After installing VS Code directly from the official website, you need to set it up for efficient Rust development.

To do this, first, launch VS Code and head to the **`Extensions`** view. Search for the "**`Rust Analyzer`**" extension, which is a must-have tool that offers intelligent code completion, inline diagnostics, and even code navigation features that empower you to write bug-free code. Once installed, VS Code will use Rust Analyzer to understand our project structure, providing suggestions and warnings that save you time during development. Along with Rust Analyzer, you may also install some other useful extensions like "Crates" which shows dependency versions in Cargo.toml and "GitLens" to help manage our repository changes directly from the IDE.

Now that Rust and VS Code are set up, it's time to fetch the essential libraries, also called crates that our project will rely on. The **`LibroCommerce`** project is our live example and serves as a modern book selling platform that we will build and refine across the book. In this initial stage, you will add several critical crates to our project through Cargo.

So, we begin by creating a new project with Cargo using:

```
cargo new libro_commerce --bin
```

This initializes a new binary project called **`libro_commerce`** with a default directory structure and a basic **`main.rs`** file. You can open this project folder in VS Code, and we will be ready to add the following essential dependencies:

- **Leptos**: The core crate that provides a reactive framework to build both server-side and client-side components in our project.
- **Tokio**: An asynchronous runtime essential for handling concurrent operations without blocking the program, ensuring that our web application scales efficiently.
- **sqlx**: A powerful, asynchronous SQL toolkit that allows you to connect to and interact with databases securely and efficiently.
- **Serde and Serde_json**: These crates handle serialization and deserialization, enabling seamless conversion of data structures into JSON format and back—a vital part of building modern, data-driven web applications.
- **Tracing and Tracing-subscriber**: Tools for structured logging and performance monitoring that give you insight into runtime behavior, crucial for troubleshooting and optimization.
- **Reqwest**: A flexible HTTP client that facilitates external API calls, perfect for integrating book metadata or payment gateways in LibroCommerce.
- **Jsonwebtoken**: Used for managing token-based authentication, ensuring that our endpoints are secure and that sensitive operations are accessible only by authorized users.
- **Argon2**: A crate dedicated to password hashing, safeguarding user credentials and other sensitive information.
- **Dotenv** (Optional): For managing environment variables securely, helping you separate configuration from code.

Just for our better understanding, the **`Cargo.toml`** dependencies section might look like this:

```
[dependencies]

leptos = "0.3"                # Check for the latest version on
crates.io

tokio = { version = "1", features = ["full"] }
```

```
sqlx = { version = "0.5", features = ["runtime-tokio-rustls",
"postgres"] }
serde = { version = "1.0", features = ["derive"] }
serde_json = "1.0"
tracing = "0.1"
tracing-subscriber = "0.2"
reqwest = { version = "0.11", features = ["json"] }
jsonwebtoken = "8"
argon2 = "0.3"
dotenv = "0.15"           # Optional, for managing
configurations
```

This gives our project the libraries it needs for a bunch of stuff, like asynchronous networking and database management, secure authentication, and real-time logging. They're each really important for making sure our app is efficient, fast, secure, and easy to extend. While you work through this, we will learn to use these crates and to link their functionalities to create a web application.

Setting up LibroCommerce Project

LibroCommerce is a book selling platform where users can browse books, view details, manage shopping carts, and complete secure transactions. This first chapter is all about setting up the environment, but it's also where you define the project's scope. We will build features bit by bit, starting with a simple interactive interface that shows server-client communication using Leptos.

When you start our new project in VS Code, we will be committing our initial setup to GitHub. If there isn't already one, we will need to set up a Git repository. To do that, simply run:

```
git init
```

Then add our project files and make our first commit:

```
git add .
git commit -m "Initial commit: Set up Rust, VS Code, and Cargo
configuration for LibroCommerce"
```

This process ensures that every change you make is tracked, and you have a reliable version control system in place. As you continue developing LibroCommerce, you will push changes to GitHub and use it to manage feature branches, merge requests, and rollback updates if necessary.

As you prepare to move forward, remember that this initial environment setup is the bedrock upon which every subsequent feature of LibroCommerce will be built. We will continue to lean on these installations and configurations in future chapters to demonstrate everything from database interactions and API creation to real-time updates and cloud deployment.

Structuring LibroCommerce App

We now roll up our sleeves and get practical about creating the GitHub repository, set up a clear branching strategy, and design a modular folder layout for our project.

Making First Commit

First, open a terminal and navigate to the location where you want our project to reside. We'll start by creating a directory for our project:

```
mkdir libro_commerce
cd libro_commerce
```

Next, initialize a local Git repository:

```
git init
```

This creates the **`.git`** folder that tracks all our changes. Now, create a basic README file to describe our project. You can do this quickly with:

```
echo "# LibroCommerce: A Modern Book Selling Platform" >
README.md
```

Now, add the README file to our Git staging area and commit the changes:

```
git add README.md
git commit -m "Initial commit: Created README for
LibroCommerce"
```

After these steps, head over to GitHub, sign in to our account, and create a new repository named **`libro_commerce`**. Once the repository is set up, link our local repository to the remote one:

```
git remote add origin
git@github.com:yourusername/libro_commerce.git
```

Finally, push our commit to GitHub:

```
git push -u origin main
```

With this, you've created our central repository and made our first commit. Our repository is now live on GitHub, and you are now able to track every change and collaborate with others.

Establishing Branching

Now that our Git repository is live, you need to set up a branching strategy. A sound strategy is to use multiple branches so that you can work on new features or bug fixes without affecting the main code. So here in our project, **main** will always contain production-ready code, and you can use a **develop** branch as an integration branch.

We start with creating a **develop** branch from **main**:

```
git checkout -b develop
git push -u origin develop
```

Now you need to remember that, for every new feature you work on, you must create a branch off of **develop**. For example, if you plan to work on the user authentication module, you can do:

```
git checkout -b feature/authentication
```

Now you can work on this feature independently. Once you finish the work and test it locally, merge our changes back into the **develop** branch with:

```
git checkout develop
git merge feature/authentication
git push origin develop
```

If you follow this workflow, you can make sure our main branch stays stable while still working on new features at the same time. You also get the benefit of using GitHub's pull request functionality, where you can review and discuss changes before merging. This reduces merge conflicts and gives you a clear history of how LibroCommerce evolves over time.

Designing Modular Folder Layout

Now, our next practical step is to organize our code with a modular folder layout. A well-organized project makes it easier for you to work on features and for future collaborators to understand our code. So here, we'll structure directories based on functionality:

```
mkdir -p src/{server,client,common}
```

```
mkdir tests config static
```

Following is a breakdown of each folder:

- **src/server** contains our backend code, including API routes, business logic, and database interactions.
- **src/client** houses our frontend code, such as Leptos components and assets that compile to WebAssembly.
- **src/common** contains shared modules like data models and utility functions that are used by both the client and server.
- **tests** is for unit and integration tests that ensure our code works as expected.
- **config** is for configuration files like environment variables, which are crucial when deploying LibroCommerce.
- **static** is a folder to store static assets like images, CSS files, and JavaScript that do not require processing.

We then create an initial **main.rs** file in the server directory:

```
touch src/server/main.rs
```

Next, we then open the **src/server/main.rs** in VS Code, and write a simple "Hello, LibroCommerce!" program to ensure our system is set up properly and well configured:

```
fn main() {
    println!("Hello, LibroCommerce!");
}
```

After you have created these files and directories, add all the changes to Git and commit them:

```
git add .
git commit -m "Set up modular folder layout and initial main.rs for LibroCommerce"
git push origin develop
```

This setup keeps things organized and makes it easy to add new features with minimal disruption. For example, if you want to work on the client-side UI, you already have a designated **src/client** directory. Similarly, any shared models or utilities go into **src/common**, and tests are kept separate in the **tests** directory.

Now here, remember that every directory you create and every branch you manage is a tool that makes our job easier. It allows you to focus on writing high-quality code and developing features that matter, rather than worrying about project chaos.

Building "Hello World" Interface

We now build a practical, Leptos-powered "Hello World" interface for our project. In this hands-on exercise, you will create a simple user interface that not only displays a greeting message but also demonstrates fundamental client–server communication. We will write code that runs on our server and compiles into WebAssembly for the browser, showing you how the Leptos framework bridges the gap between robust Rust backend processes and dynamic, interactive frontend experiences. By working through this example, you gain both confidence and a real-world demonstration of how to move ideas into a live project.

Setting up Project

Before we dive into the code, make sure you've already set up the LibroCommerce repository and created the modular folder layout, as we mentioned before. First, open our project in VS Code, and navigate to the **`/src/client`** directory where our Leptos components reside. In this project, we will create a new component file (let's call it **`hello.rs`**) that serves as our starting point for the interface. This file will contain a simple Leptos component that renders "Hello, LibroCommerce!" to the user.

Writing Leptos Component

Now, we access the **`src/client/hello.rs`** file in VS Code and add following code:

```
use leptos::*;
// Define our HelloWorld component.
#[component]
pub fn HelloWorld(cx: Scope) -> Element {
    view! { cx,
        <div>
            <h1>"Hello, LibroCommerce!"</h1>
            <p>"Welcome to our first interactive Leptos
interface."</p>
        </div>
    }
```

```
}
```

In this code, you are using Leptos' **view!** macro to declare a component that renders HTML elements directly into the browser. The **#[component]** attribute makes this function a reactive component. This is a fundamental building block that will allow you to integrate more advanced features later on.

Integrating Component into App

With our **HelloWorld** component ready, the next practical step is to integrate it into the client-side application so that it's visible when you run our project. So here, we now create a new file, say **src/client/lib.rs**, which serves as the main entry point for compiling our WebAssembly modules. In this file, you should set up the Leptos runtime and mount our component to a specific HTML element in the DOM.

Following is a quick code for **lib.rs**:

```
use leptos::*;
mod hello; // Import our HelloWorld component from hello.rs
#[wasm_bindgen(start)]
pub fn start() {
    // This will mount our component to the <body> element.
    mount_to_body(|cx| view! { cx,
        <hello::HelloWorld />
    });
}
```

This above uses the **wasm_bindgen** attribute to declare a function that runs when the WebAssembly module is loaded in the browser. By calling **mount_to_body**, we instruct Leptos to render our **HelloWorld** component within the HTML document's **<body>**. This step effectively bridges the gap between our Rust server-side logic and the modern, interactive client-side experience provided by Leptos.

Demonstrating Basic Client–Server Communication

While our "Hello World" interface is simple, it's also an excellent opportunity to introduce basic client–server communication. In a full-fledged application, you would typically fetch data from the server and update our UI accordingly. For now, let's simulate this concept by adding a simple asynchronous function that mimics fetching a greeting message from the server.

To do this, access the **src/server/main.rs** file and add the following function:

```
use leptos::*;
use tokio::runtime::Runtime;
// Simple simulated server function that returns a greeting message.
pub async fn fetch_greeting() -> String {
    "Hello, LibroCommerce from the server!".to_string()
}
fn main() {
    // Create a runtime to execute our async code.
    let rt = Runtime::new().unwrap();
    let greeting = rt.block_on(fetch_greeting());
    println!("{}", greeting);
}
```

This above function introduces you to asynchronous programming with Rust and the Tokio runtime in order to support non-blocking operations. Although this server-side function is quite basic, it demonstrates a key principle: how our server can prepare data to be sent to the client. In real scenarios, you would build an API that the frontend calls, and the data fetched from the server could be used to update our Leptos components. By running our server code, we will see the greeting printed in our terminal.

Compiling and Running Leptos App

Now that the codes are in place for both client and server components, we now compile and run our application. For this, we first navigate to the project directory in the terminal and build the project:

```
cargo build --target wasm32-unknown-unknown
```

Next, you will need to serve the compiled WebAssembly file along with an HTML file that loads our app. A simple way to do this is by using a static file server for which you create an **index.html** file in our **static** folder with the following content:

```
<!DOCTYPE html>
<html lang="en">
```

```
<head>
    <meta charset="UTF-8">
    <title>LibroCommerce</title>
</head>
<body>
    <script type="module">
        import init from './libro_commerce_bg.wasm';
        init();
    </script>
</body>
</html>
```

The above HTML file is designed to load our compiled WebAssembly module. You can now use a simple static file server maybe something like Python's HTTP server to serve this file.

After this, run the following:

```
python3 -m http.server 8080 --directory static
```

Once done, open the browser and navigate to **`http://localhost:8080`**. You should see our Leptos "Hello World" interface displaying "Hello, LibroCommerce!" along with a welcome message. This confirms that our client-side code has been successfully compiled to WebAssembly, loaded in the browser, and that the basic client–server communication (via our simulation) is in place.

So, with this, you now have a working base that highlights the seamless integration of Rust's performance and safety with Leptos' dynamic front-end capabilities.

Summary

In short, you set up a solid development environment for LibroCommerce, a modern book selling platform. You installed Rust using Cargo on a Linux system and configured VS Code with Rust Analyzer to enhance our coding workflow. You added key Rust crates like Leptos, Tokio, sqlx, Serde, and others into our project, setting the stage for building a reactive, high-performance web application. You got things started with a Git repository, set up a GitHub repository, and came up with effective branching strategies that let you develop features safely. You created a modular folder layout to separate server, client, and shared code, which made project management way easier.

And finally, you got that "Hello World" interface with Leptos to show a simple greeting and prove basic client-server communication using asynchronous calls. You confirmed our setup by compiling the code to WebAssembly and running it through a local static file server, making sure that the client-side interface integrated seamlessly with the backend. These handy steps let you try out industry-standard tools like VS Code and GitHub and set up the basic framework and workflow needed to build advanced web apps using modern techniques.

CHAPTER 2: DESIGNING MODERN ARCHITECTURE

Overview

This chapter's going to start by looking at some current design patterns and microservice ideas that are behind today's web apps and why having a modular design can improve things like how easily they can be used by more people at the same time and how they can be made more resistant to problems. Then, we will create clear service boundaries for LibroCommerce by splitting the codebase into three main modules—inventory, orders, and user accounts. We will use VS Code's project management features to make navigation and debugging easier.

Next, we will define shared data models, build HTTP handlers with Axum, and develop Leptos components that fetch and render data, mapping complete client–server–database flows through concrete user journeys. Finally, we will integrate structured logging and error monitoring using the Tracing ecosystem, configure a global subscriber with dynamic filtering, apply TraceLayer for automatic request spans, and annotate handlers for detailed diagnostics. By the chapter's end, we will have a solid architecture that supports modular development and interactive UIs. It'll also give you real-time visibility into app behavior and errors, so you can establish a strong base for building and maintaining a top-notch web platform.

Modern Web Concepts

These days, web app design isn't limited to one big architecture where all the features are crammed into a single codebase. Instead, the industry has moved towards a modular mindset, where responsibilities are clearly divided between loosely coupled components. You've seen how design patterns like Model-View-Controller (MVC) have changed over time, and now we're working with patterns that focus on separation of concerns, reusable components, and autonomous services. These patterns help you develop code that's easier to test, maintain, and extend as our application grows. For example, you could use a component-based architecture in the frontend with frameworks like Leptos. This allows for modular UI development and makes it easy to see the connection between state and presentation. Each part of the application is responsible for its own tasks, which makes it more flexible and adaptable to changing needs. As you adopt these approaches, we will be leveraging not only clean coding principles but also making sure that every part of our system interacts harmoniously. This will reduce technical debt in the long run and enable you to iterate on features quickly.

Microservices for Modern Apps

Lately, microservices have become a key part of web development. With microservices, you can break down complex applications into smaller, independent services that communicate via lightweight protocols. In a microservices architecture, each service is built around a specific business capability. For example, there's a dedicated module for handling user authentication, another for managing product inventory, and yet another for processing payments. This makes our system more resilient since the failure of one service is isolated and doesn't bring down the whole application. You can work on, test, and deploy each service on its own, which leads to quicker development cycles and faster release times. As you design LibroCommerce, we will benefit from separating its functionalities into distinct services. One service might manage the book catalog, while another handles orders, and another oversees user reviews. This strategy makes the development process more efficient and flexible, allowing you to scale parts of our application independently. Since each microservice talks to other services using clearly defined interfaces, you can also add new technologies, update existing services, or replace parts without messing up the whole system.

Modern Architecture for better UX

The whole point of adopting these modern design strategies is to improve the end-user experience. When you divide our application into smaller, independent parts, you can make each part do its specific job better. For example, if a service handles real-time data, like updating book availability or processing orders, the responsiveness and efficiency of that module directly enhance user interaction. We will get to design interfaces that react instantly to user input, and that's key in today's fast-paced digital environments. Picture this: a user browsing our LibroCommerce app. With a well-structured microservices architecture, the catalog pages load quickly, order data is fetched seamlessly from a dedicated service, and real-time notifications guide the user experience. This all-in-one approach makes sure that user interactions are smooth and the overall performance stays solid, even when our application scales to handle a lot of users at once. When you design our system like this, every microservice and component is optimized for technical excellence and for delivering real benefits to the end-user.

Key Architectural Patterns

When you keep going on this project, we will come across all kinds of architectural patterns that go along with modern web development practices. One example is event-driven architecture, where services react to events or changes in state in real time. For LibroCommerce, you might have a system that responds right away when a new book is added to the inventory or when a user finishes a purchase. We will also explore strategies like API Gateway patterns, which centralize and simplify client communications with multiple backend services. When we built LibroCommerce, we used these patterns to make sure that every interaction, from browsing the catalog to checking out, is supported by a design that's built for top performance and reliability. As you integrate these patterns into our project, we will start to see how the combined benefits of scalability, fault tolerance, and reduced inter-service dependencies contribute to a better user experience. Our app will be able to handle more traffic and provide a more stable and interactive experience that keeps users engaged.

So, you've laid the groundwork for designing a modern architecture for LibroCommerce. It's all about the latest trends in design patterns and microservice strategies. We will dive into how these patterns have totally changed the game for web applications, how they make the user experience better, and how these modular, independent services team up to create reliable, scalable, and efficient systems. These insights will help you apply architectural principles to our development journey, making sure that every feature of our application is built on a solid foundation that can handle the future. This deep dive into modern web architecture will show you how to create dynamic, resilient, and user-centric applications.

Setting Up Modules and Service Boundaries

Now that you've got a good handle on the latest design patterns, we will learn how to break our project into logical sections. It makes development easier and makes it easier to maintain and expand in the future. We'll create a modular structure that makes it easy to develop, test, and integrate each part of our application smoothly.

So now to begin, we need to identify the key functionalities our book selling platform will support. For LibroCommerce, three essential modules have emerged: the Inventory module, which handles book listings and catalog management; the Orders module, which manages shopping carts, order processing, and transactions; and the User Accounts module, which deals with user registration, authentication, and profile management. This separation allows you to focus on individual areas of business logic without worrying about unwanted interdependencies. For example, imagine you are updating the mechanism for displaying book details in the Inventory module. With clear module separation, this update can be performed without disrupting the user authentication system in the User Accounts module.

Creating Modules in Project Structure

Let's move from concept to practice. At first, navigate to our **src** directory. Here, you will create new subdirectories for each module and run the following:

```
mkdir -p src/{inventory,orders,user_accounts}
```

This will create three subdirectories—**inventory**, **orders**, and **user_accounts**—each representing a distinct part of LibroCommerce's functionality. In each directory, we will create an initial **mod.rs** file that acts as the entry point for that module. For instance, create a file in the inventory folder by navigating into it and then running:

```
cd src/inventory
touch mod.rs
```

You need to repeat similar steps for the orders and user_accounts directories. The **mod.rs** files will define the public interface of our modules and can later be expanded with specific functions, data structures, and business logic.

Writing Modules

Let's add some simple code to each module to illustrate the structure. It starts with editing the **src/inventory/mod.rs** file with the following edits:

```
// src/inventory/mod.rs
pub fn list_books() -> Vec<&'static str> {
    vec!["Book A", "Book B", "Book C"]
}
```

This simulates listing books available in our catalog. Next, then open **src/orders/mod.rs** and add:

```
// src/orders/mod.rs
pub fn create_order(user_id: u32, book_ids: Vec<u32>) -> String {
    format!("Order created for user {} with books: {:?}", user_id, book_ids)
}
```

And finally, in **src/user_accounts/mod.rs**, add:

```
// src/user_accounts/mod.rs
pub fn register_user(username: &str, email: &str) -> String {
    format!("User '{}' with email '{}' has been registered.", username, email)
}
```

This modular design allows you to test and extend each part independently. These examples serve as placeholders that you will build on later as you implement actual business logic for LibroCommerce.

Integrating Modules

And since our project is split into separate modules, you can use VS Code's built-in features to quickly find and change code segments. The "Explorer" panel, for example, clearly shows our folder structure, making it a breeze to switch between modules. You can use the "Search" function (Ctrl+Shift+F) to find function names, references, or even specific strings across our whole project. This makes sure that each module communicates properly with others.

The integrated terminal in VS Code lets you run our application and tests without leaving the editor, making our workflow more streamlined. You can also use VS Code's debugging tools to step through code in any module, inspect variables, and watch function calls interact as you simulate various functionalities of LibroCommerce. For example, if you want to test the list_books function in the Inventory module, you can quickly write a test case in our tests directory and run it directly from within VS Code, observing output in real time. With this integration, collaborating is a breeze since each module's role is clearly defined and easy to follow.

Connecting Modules

Now that you have individual modules, the next step is to connect them into a cohesive application. To do this, acess the **`src/main.rs`** and import our modules using the **`mod`** keyword and call their functions to see their interaction. For our better understanding, the **`src/main.rs`** might look like this:

```
mod inventory;

mod orders;

mod user_accounts;

fn main() {

    // Use the inventory module to list books.

    let books = inventory::list_books();

    println!("Available Books: {:?}", books);

    // Simulate registering a new user with the user_accounts
module.

    let registration_message =
user_accounts::register_user("Alice", "alice@example.com");

    println!("{}", registration_message);

    // Create a sample order using the orders module.

    let order = orders::create_order(1, vec![101, 102]);

    println!("{}", order);

}
```

After this, run the **`cargo run`** and it will let you see how the modules interact. This is a critical step: seeing the integration in action validates our modular approach and confirms that each part of the system is ready to be expanded with more complex functionality.

This whole task simplifies managing our project's complexity and also form a replicable process for any future GitHub project.

Visualizing Data Flows and User Journeys

After building the clear module boundaries for **`inventory`**, **`orders`**, and **`user_accounts`**, we now look into exactly how data travels through our LibroCommerce app. What we are going to do here is we will wire each module into HTTP endpoints, consume them with Leptos components, and walk through two concrete user journeys. The user journeys can be browsing the catalog and placing an order.

Reviewing Modules and Service Boundaries

So far, we have already created 3 Rust modules under **`src/`**:

- **inventory** with **`list_books()`**
- **user_accounts** with **`register_user()`**
- **orders** with **`create_order()`**

Each module lives in its own folder (**`src/inventory`**, **`src/user_accounts`**, **`src/orders`**) and exposes a simple function. Now we will expose those functions over HTTP so that the client can consume them.

Implementing HTTP Handlers for Each Module

We first begin to create **`src/server/handlers.rs`** and add handlers that call our module functions:

```
// src/server/handlers.rs
use axum::{Json, extract::Path};
use common::models::{Book, User, Order};
use inventory;
use user_accounts;
use orders;
// GET /api/books
pub async fn books_handler() -> Json<Vec<String>> {
    // calls inventory::list_books()
    Json(inventory::list_books())
}
// POST /api/register/:username/:email
```

```
pub async fn register_handler(Path((username, email)):
Path<(String, String)>) -> Json<String> {
    Json(user_accounts::register_user(&username, &email))
}
// POST /api/order/:user_id/:book_ids
pub async fn order_handler(Path((user_id, book_ids)):
Path<(u32, String)>) -> Json<String> {
    // parse comma-separated book IDs
    let ids: Vec<u32> = book_ids
        .split(',')
        .filter_map(|s| s.parse().ok())
        .collect();
    Json(orders::create_order(user_id, ids))
}
```

Then wire these into an Axum router in **src/server/main.rs**:

```
// src/server/main.rs
use axum::{routing::{get, post}, Router};
use std::net::SocketAddr;
mod handlers;
#[tokio::main]
async fn main() {
    let app = Router::new()
        .route("/api/books", get(handlers::books_handler))
        .route("/api/register/:username/:email",
post(handlers::register_handler))
        .route("/api/order/:user_id/:book_ids",
post(handlers::order_handler));
    let addr = SocketAddr::from(([127, 0, 0, 1], 3000));
    println!("Server running on {}", addr);
```

```
axum::Server::bind(&addr).serve(app.into_make_service()).await
.unwrap();
}
```

At this point, each module function is reachable via HTTP, forming the "server" half of our data flow.

Crafting Leptos Components

On the client side, we will create corresponding Leptos components in **src/client** for each module:

- BookList Component

```
// src/client/book_list.rs
use leptos::*;
#[component]
pub fn BookList(cx: Scope) -> Element {
    let books = create_signal(cx, Vec::<String>::new());
    spawn_local(async move {
        let fetched: Vec<String> =
            reqwest::get("/api/books")
            .await.unwrap()
            .json().await.unwrap();
        books.set(fetched);
    });
    view! { cx,
        <ul>
            {books.get().iter().map(|b| view! { cx,
<li>{b.clone()}</li> }).collect::<Vec<_>>()}
        </ul>
    }
}
```

- RegisterForm Component

```
// src/client/register_form.rs
use leptos::*;
#[component]
pub fn RegisterForm(cx: Scope) -> Element {
    let username = create_signal(cx, "".to_string());
    let email = create_signal(cx, "".to_string());
    let message = create_signal(cx, "".to_string());
    let on_submit = move |_| {
        let u = username.get().clone();
        let e = email.get().clone();
        spawn_local(async move {
            let resp: String =
                reqwest::Client::new()
                .post(format!("/api/register/{}/{}", u, e))
                .send().await.unwrap()
                .text().await.unwrap();
            message.set(resp);
        });
    };
    view! { cx,
        <form on:submit=on_submit>
            <input type="text" placeholder="Username"
on:input=move |ev| username.set(event_target_value(&ev)) />
            <input type="email" placeholder="Email"
on:input=move |ev| email.set(event_target_value(&ev)) />
            <button type="submit">"Register"</button>
        </form>
        <p>{message.get()}</p>
    }
```

```
}
```

- OrderButton Component

```
// src/client/order_button.rs
use leptos::*;
#[component]
pub fn OrderButton(cx: Scope, user_id: u32, book_id: u32) ->
Element {
    let status = create_signal(cx, "".to_string());
    let on_click = move |_| {
        spawn_local(async move {
            let resp: String =
                reqwest::Client::new()
                .post(format!("/api/order/{}/{}", user_id,
book_id))
                .send().await.unwrap()
                .text().await.unwrap();
            status.set(resp);
        });
    };
    view! { cx,
        <div>
          <button on:click=on_click>"Add to Cart"</button>
          <p>{status.get()}</p>
        </div>
    }
}
```

All these components directly consume our server endpoints, thereby completing the “client” half of the data path.

Mapping End-to-end Data Path

Now we will connect the dots for the **"Browse Books"** journey:

- Page Load
  - Leptos mounts **<BookList/>**.
- HTTP Request
  - **reqwest::get("/api/books")** is issued.
- Axum Handler
  - **books_handler** calls **inventory::list_books()**.
- Module Function
  - **list_books()** returns a **Vec<String>**.
- HTTP Response
  - Axum serializes as JSON.
- Client Update
  - Leptos sets the **books** signal and re-renders the **<ul>**.

For the **"Register & Order"** journey:

- User Submits Form
  - **RegisterForm** sends POST **/api/register/<user>/<email>**.
- Axum Handler
  - **register_handler** calls **user_accounts::register_user()**.
- Module Function
  - Returns confirmation **String**.
- Client Update
  - Leptos displays the message.
- User Clicks "Add to Cart"
  - **<OrderButton/>** triggers POST **/api/order/<user_id>/<book_id>**.
- Axum Handler
  - **order_handler** calls **orders::create_order()**.
- Module Function
  - Returns order confirmation.

- Client Update
    - Leptos shows order status.

We can also utilize the VS Code's features to follow these flows:

- Go to **Definition** on **list_books**, **register_user**, **create_order**.
- **Peek References** on **/api/books** in our router.
- **Breakpoint** in **books_handler**, run our server (**cargo run**), and reload the browser to inspect variables.
- **Debug Client** by serving our WebAssembly bundle and setting breakpoints in **spawn_local** callbacks.

With this, you very well mapped how data is defined in shared models, exposed through server handlers, called our modular functions, and finally rendered for the user. If you picture these data paths and how users go through them, you can see the whole process from the user interface to the database and back.

Integrating Logging and Monitoring

In this last topic, we will instrument our app with the **Tracing** crate to add structured logging and error capturing. It will activate real-time diagnostics that help us to trace requests, measure latency, and catch errors as they occur. All code lives in our server module. There are no frontend changes necessary for basic logging. We can immediately see HTTP requests and internal events logged to the console or to a file.

Adding Tracing Dependencies

To begin with, we add the necessary crates to our **Cargo.toml** under the **[dependencies]** section:

```
tracing = "0.1"
tracing-subscriber = { version = "0.3", features = ["env-filter", "fmt", "json"] }
```

Here, **tracing** provides the macros and types for instrumentation, and the **tracing-subscriber** offers subscribers to collect and format tracing data, including console output and environment-controlled filtering. We then run the **cargo update** or **cargo build** to fetch and compile these new dependencies.

Initializing Tracing Subscriber

Next, we then configure a global subscriber in our **src/server/main.rs** before building the Axum router. We simply replace the existing **main** with the following:

```
use axum::{routing::{get, post}, Router};
use std::net::SocketAddr;
use tracing_subscriber::{fmt, EnvFilter, layer::SubscriberExt,
util::SubscriberInitExt};
mod handlers;
#[tokio::main]
async fn main() {
    // 1. Set up an environment filter (LOG_LEVEL env var;
default INFO).
    let filter = EnvFilter::try_from_default_env()
        .unwrap_or_else(|_| EnvFilter::new("info"));
    // 2. Build a subscriber with formatted, JSON, and filter
layers.
    fmt()
        .json()                         // JSON output for
structured logs
        .with_env_filter(filter)       // Filter based on
RUST_LOG
        .init();                       // Install as global
default
    // 3. Define routes as before.
    let app = Router::new()
        .route("/api/books", get(handlers::books_handler))
        .route("/api/register/:username/:email",
post(handlers::register_handler))
        .route("/api/order/:user_id/:book_ids",
post(handlers::order_handler));
    let addr = SocketAddr::from(([127, 0, 0, 1], 3000));
    tracing::info!(%addr, "Starting LibroCommerce server");
    axum::Server::bind(&addr)
```

```
        .serve(app.into_make_service())
        .await
        .unwrap();
}
```

Here, the **EnvFilter** reads a **RUST_LOG** environment variable (e.g., **export RUST_LOG=debug**) to control verbosity. The **fmt().json()** outputs logs as JSON lines, enabling easy parsing by log aggregators, and the **tracing::info!** logs the server start event with structured fields.

Instrumenting HTTP Handlers

Now to automatically trace each request, we wrap our router in a **TraceLayer**. Add the **tower-http** crate:

```
tower-http = { version = "0.3", features = ["trace"] }
```

Then we modify **main.rs**:

```
use tower_http::trace::TraceLayer;
// ...
let app = Router::new()
    .route("/api/books", get(handlers::books_handler))
    .route("/api/register/:username/:email",
post(handlers::register_handler))
    .route("/api/order/:user_id/:book_ids",
post(handlers::order_handler))
    .layer(
        TraceLayer::new_for_http()
            .make_span_with(|request: &http::Request<_>| {
                tracing::info_span!(
                    "http_request",
                    method = %request.method(),
                    uri = %request.uri()
                )
```

```
            })
    );
```

This layer creates a tracing span for each incoming HTTP request, and logs method, URI, status code, and response time automatically.

Adding Logging Inside Handlers and Modules

Now here, we need to remember that within our handlers, we sprinkle **tracing::debug!**, **tracing::info!**, and **tracing::error!** calls to capture significant events or errors.

To do this, we edit the following in **src/server/handlers.rs**:

```
use axum::{Json, extract::Path};
use serde_json::json;
use common::models::{Book};
use inventory;
use tracing::{instrument, error, info};
#[instrument(skip_all)]
pub async fn books_handler() -> Json<Vec<String>> {
    info!("Fetching book list from inventory module");
    match inventory::list_books() {
        books => {
            info!(count = books.len(), "Successfully retrieved
books");
            Json(books)
        }
    }
}
#[instrument(skip(Path))]
pub async fn register_handler(Path((username, email)):
Path<(String, String)>) -> Json<String> {
    info!(user = %username, "Registering new user");
    let result = user_accounts::register_user(&username,
&email);
```

```
    info!("User registration successful");
    Json(result)
}
#[instrument(skip(Path))]
pub async fn order_handler(Path((user_id, book_ids)):
Path<(u32, String)>) -> Json<String> {
    info!(user_id, "Creating order");
    let ids: Vec<u32> = book_ids
        .split(',')
        .filter_map(|s| s.parse().ok())
        .collect();
    let order = orders::create_order(user_id, ids);
    info!(order = %order, "Order created");
    Json(order)
}
```

Here, **#[instrument]** automatically records function arguments and enters a new span. The **info!** calls annotate progress; **error!** logs failures. And combined with **TraceLayer**, we get end-to-end visibility for each request.

Capturing and Reporting Errors

To catch and log panics or unexpected errors in asynchronous contexts, we simply install the **tracing-error** crate:

```
tracing-error = "0.2"
```

Then we wrap our **main** body with error handling:

```
use tracing_error::ErrorLayer;
use tracing_subscriber::Registry;
// Build a subscriber with an error layer
let subscriber = Registry::default()
    .with(filter)
    .with(fmt::layer().json())
```

```
    .with(ErrorLayer::default());
subscriber.init();
// In our async context, use `tracing_error::ResultExt`
let result = some_async_operation().await.context("Some
operation failed");
if let Err(e) = result {
    error!(error = %e, "Operation encountered an error");
}
```

This setup captures backtraces on errors, attaches context messages via **`.context()`**, and logs full error chains.

If you want to see the logs in real time, simply run the following on our server:

```
export RUST_LOG=debug
cargo run
```

The logs will appear in JSON or human-readable format depending on our subscriber config. In VS Code's **`Terminal`** panel, you can search and filter logs.

With all this work around, you gain full visibility into every request, database call, and internal operation. You can now diagnose issues, measure performance, and ensure that LibroCommerce runs smoothly under all conditions.

Summary

During the chapter, you learned how web apps have changed from being all-in-one to modular, with an emphasis on keeping things separate and reusing parts. You learned that microservices break functionality into independent services, like inventory, orders, and user accounts. This makes the application more resilient, scalable, and easier to maintain. You basically created those modules in our filesystem, added sample functions, and used VS Code's project explorer and integrated terminal to navigate, test, and debug each component.

Later, you then defined shared data models for books, users, and orders, and built HTTP handlers using Axum that exposed those models over REST endpoints. On the client side, you developed Leptos components—like BookList, RegisterForm, and OrderButton—to consume these endpoints and render dynamic content. You mapped out the data flows from start to finish, following each HTTP request from the browser to the database and back, and walked through specific user journeys for browsing the catalog and placing an order. At last, you added the Tracing crate and tracing-subscriber to our server, set up a global subscriber with an EnvFilter and JSON formatter, applied a TraceLayer to capture spans for every request, and annotated handlers with #[instrument] and log macros. You also integrated the ErrorLayer to capture backtraces and contextual error information. With these handy steps, we will be able to make real-time diagnostics, organized logging, and solid error reporting part of a web application that's ready to go in production.

CHAPTER 3: BUILDING APPLICATION SERVER

Overview

This chapter starts by setting up an asynchronous runtime with Tokio and setting up Axum routes that extract path parameters for dynamic endpoints. It'll let you combine Leptos to work with server-driven components and API handlers in the same application. Then, we will set up our back end with dedicated modules for inventory management, order processing via SQLX transactions, and payment workflows using REQWEST. The plan is to add a metadata module that retrieves book details from an external API and makes them available over HTTP.

Next, we will set up our server with the Tracing ecosystem, starting with a subscriber with JSON output and environment-based filters, and adding a TraceLayer to capture request spans. We will use jsonwebtoken to validate JWTs, extract user claims, and protect key routes. As you go through the chapter, we will be writing, testing, and observing code in VS Code to make sure every component, from routing to authentication, is working right. By that time, we will have a production-grade application server that can handle concurrent connections, integrate third-party services, and provide real-time diagnostics and security for LibroCommerce.

Building Responsive Web Server with Tokio

We now look into why dynamic routing and concurrent request handling are essential for modern web applications and then build a high-performance server using Tokio as the asynchronous runtime and Axum for routing. Leptos will be used to render server-driven pages or APIs as needed. We can explore how these components work together to handle multiple user requests simultaneously, route parameters dynamically, and maintain a responsive experience for every user.

Dynamic Routing and Concurrent Requests

Dynamic routing allows our server to respond to URLs containing variable segments—such as **`/book/42`**—by extracting parameters at runtime rather than hard-coding every possible path. It helps to gain flexibility to serve resources based on user input, session data, or database lookups. Concurrent request handling ensures that our server can process multiple HTTP connections at once without blocking on slow operations like database queries, file I/O, or external API calls. The use of Tokio's non-blocking, event-driven model helps to avoid thread-per-connection limits and achieve high throughput. In a production scenario, dozens or hundreds of users might browse LibroCommerce's catalog, place orders, and fetch user profiles at the same time.

We learned previously that Tokio provides the foundational runtime that powers asynchronous Rust applications. It uses a work-stealing executor to run lightweight tasks, multiplexing thousands of concurrent operations across a small number of OS threads. When you annotate our **`main`** function with **`#[tokio::main]`**, you automatically get a multi-threaded runtime capable of spawning tasks via **`tokio::spawn`**. Combining this with Axum's router, which is built on

Tower and Tokio, you obtain a server that can dispatch requests, await asynchronous operations, and return responses without ever blocking the event loop. This architecture translates directly into better resource utilization and improved responsiveness, especially under heavy load. Every database call, file read, or external HTTP request runs as an asynchronous future, allowing other tasks to proceed until it completes.

Implementing Dynamic Routes with Axum

S now, to demonstrate dynamic routing, we will create parameterized endpoints that extract path variables. In our **`src/server/main.rs`**, we at first import the necessary modules and define routes like **`/api/book/:id`** and **`/api/user/:username`** as below:

```
use axum::{
    extract::Path,
    routing::get,
    Router,
    Json
};
use tokio;
use std::net::SocketAddr;
use common::models::Book;
mod inventory;
async fn root() -> &'static str {
    "Welcome to LibroCommerce!"
}
async fn get_book(Path(id): Path<i32>) -> Json<Book> {
    // Simulate fetching from inventory module
    let book = inventory::find_book(id).await;
    Json(book)
}
async fn list_books() -> Json<Vec<Book>> {
    let books = inventory::list_books().await;
    Json(books)
```

```
}
#[tokio::main]
async fn main() {
    let app = Router::new()
        .route("/", get(root))
        .route("/api/books", get(list_books))
        .route("/api/book/:id", get(get_book));
    let addr = SocketAddr::from(([127, 0, 0, 1], 3000));
    println!("Server listening on {}", addr);
    axum::Server::bind(&addr)
        .serve(app.into_make_service())
        .await
        .unwrap();
}
```

Here, the **Path(id): Path<i32>** dynamically extracts the integer **id** from the URL. This pattern applies to any parameterized route.

Ensuring Concurrency and Responsiveness

Since each handler is **async**, multiple requests can execute concurrently. For example, if one user requests **/api/book/1** and another requests **/api/books** at the same moment, Tokio schedules both futures on its thread pool. When **inventory::find_book(id).await** is pending on a database query, the runtime picks up the other future and runs it without delay. This non-blocking behavior ensures that slow operations—like a complex SQL join—do not stall the entire server.

To further enhance responsiveness, you can spawn background tasks for long-running jobs:

```
tokio::spawn(async move {
    inventory::update_cache().await;
});
```

This line fires off a cache-refresh job without affecting the current request's flow.

Integrating Leptos for Server-Driven Pages

If you intend to serve SSR pages, you can integrate Leptos rendering within an Axum handler. For example, to render a homepage using Leptos:

```
use leptos::*;
use leptos_axum::{LeptosRoutes, generate_route_list};
mod app; // our Leptos root component
#[tokio::main]
async fn main() {
    let routes = generate_route_list(|cx| view! { cx,
<app::App/> });
    let leptos_options = get_leptos_options();
    let app = Router::new()
        .leptos_routes(&leptos_options, routes)
        .into_make_service();
    axum::Server::bind(&addr).serve(app).await.unwrap();
}
```

This lets you handle both dynamic API routing and server-side rendered pages within the same Tokio runtime and Leptos framework for consistent Rust code across our stack.

Testing and Observing Performance

After implementing our server, you can stress-test endpoints using tools such as **ab** (ApacheBench) or **wrk**. For instance:

```
wrk -t4 -c100 -d30s http://localhost:3000/api/books
```

This command opens 100 concurrent connections with 4 threads over 30 seconds, measuring latency and throughput. You should observe low average response times and high requests per second, thanks to Tokio's concurrency model.

With all this, you can now certainly handle parameterized URLs, process concurrent HTTP requests without blocking, and render interactive pages—all within a unified, high-performance Rust tech stack.

Implementing Business Logic

With our responsive server in place, we will now develop the core backend modules that power LibroCommerce's key features: listing books, managing orders, and handling payments. Each module lives under **src/server**, uses the shared data models, and interacts with our database or external services. We will write asynchronous functions using **sqlx** for database operations and **reqwest** for payment gateway calls.

Inventory Module: Fetching and Filtering Books

First, we begin with creating **src/server/inventory.rs** and implement functions to list and search books:

```
// src/server/inventory.rs
use sqlx::PgPool;
use common::models::Book;
use tracing::instrument;
/// Retrieves all books from the database.
#[instrument(skip(pool))]
pub async fn list_books(pool: &PgPool) ->
sqlx::Result<Vec<Book>> {
    sqlx::query_as!(
        Book,
        r#"
        SELECT id, title, author, price
        FROM books
        ORDER BY title
        "#
    )
    .fetch_all(pool)
    .await
}
/// Searches books by title keyword.
#[instrument(skip(pool))]
pub async fn search_books(pool: &PgPool, keyword: &str) ->
sqlx::Result<Vec<Book>> {
```

```
    let pattern = format!("%{}%", keyword);
    sqlx::query_as!(
        Book,
        r#"
        SELECT id, title, author, price
        FROM books
        WHERE title ILIKE $1
        ORDER BY title
        "#,
        pattern
    )
    .fetch_all(pool)
    .await
}
```

Here, we passed a **PgPool** reference to share connections. The **#[instrument]** macro logs function entry, arguments, and execution time. And, the **list_books** returns all books, and **search_books** filters by title.

Creating and Managing Orders

Within the **src/server/orders.rs**, we implement order creation, status checking, and stock updates:

```
// src/server/orders.rs
use sqlx::{PgPool, Postgres, Transaction};
use common::models::Order;
use tracing::{instrument, error};
/// Creates an order: inserts row, updates inventory, returns
Order.
#[instrument(skip(pool))]
pub async fn create_order(
    pool: &PgPool,
```

```
    user_id: i32,
    book_ids: Vec<i32>,
) -> Result<Order, sqlx::Error> {
    let mut tx: Transaction<'_, Postgres> =
pool.begin().await?;

    // Calculate total price
    let mut total = 0.0;
    for &book_id in &book_ids {
        let rec: (f64,) = sqlx::query_as("SELECT price FROM
books WHERE id = $1")
            .bind(book_id)
            .fetch_one(&mut tx)
            .await?;
        total += rec.0;
        // Decrement stock
        sqlx::query("UPDATE books SET stock = stock - 1 WHERE
id = $1 AND stock > 0")
            .bind(book_id)
            .execute(&mut tx)
            .await?;
    }

    // Insert order record
    let order = sqlx::query_as!(
        Order,
        r#"
        INSERT INTO orders (user_id, book_ids, total)
        VALUES ($1, $2, $3)
        RETURNING id, user_id, book_ids, total
```

```
        "#,
        user_id,
        &book_ids,
        total
    )
    .fetch_one(&mut tx)
    .await?;

    tx.commit().await?;
    Ok(order)
}
/// Retrieves an existing order by ID.
#[instrument(skip(pool))]
pub async fn get_order(pool: &PgPool, order_id: i32) ->
Result<Order, sqlx::Error> {
    sqlx::query_as!(
        Order,
        "SELECT id, user_id, book_ids, total FROM orders WHERE
id = $1",
        order_id
    )
    .fetch_one(pool)
    .await
}
```

Here, the **transaction** groups price calculation, stock update, and insertion, ensuring atomicity. And, the **`get_order`** fetches a single order.

Integrating External Payment Gateways

We then integrate a real payment provider in **`src/server/payments.rs`**:

```
// src/server/payments.rs
```

```
use reqwest::Client;
use serde::Deserialize;
use tracing::{instrument, error};
#[derive(Deserialize)]
struct PaymentResponse {
    success: bool,
    transaction_id: String,
}
/// Processes payment by calling an external API.
#[instrument(skip(client, amount, card_token))]
pub async fn process_payment(
    client: &Client,
    amount: f64,
    card_token: &str,
) -> Result<String, reqwest::Error> {
    let resp = client
        .post("https://api.paymentprovider.com/charge")
        .json(&serde_json::json!({
            "amount": amount,
            "currency": "USD",
            "token": card_token
        }))
        .send()
        .await?;

    if !resp.status().is_success() {
        error!(status = %resp.status(), "Payment API returned
error");
        return Err(reqwest::Error::new(
            reqwest::StatusCode::BAD_REQUEST,
```

```
            "Payment failed",
        ));
    }

    let body: PaymentResponse = resp.json().await?;
    if body.success {
        Ok(body.transaction_id)
    } else {
        error!("Payment was declined by provider");
        Err(reqwest::Error::new(
            reqwest::StatusCode::PAYMENT_REQUIRED,
            "Payment declined",
        ))
    }
}
```

Here,

- We used **reqwest::Client** for HTTP calls, passing JSON payloads.
- Then the structured logging records HTTP status and errors.
- Upon success, you returned the transaction ID for order confirmation.

Composing Handlers for Business Logic

And then finally, we update our HTTP handlers in **src/server/handlers.rs** to invoke these modules:

```
// src/server/handlers.rs
use axum::{extract::{Path, Json, State}, http::StatusCode};
use sqlx::PgPool;
use reqwest::Client;
use common::models::{Book, Order};
use inventory;
```

```rust
use orders;
use payments;
use tracing::instrument;
pub struct AppState {
    pub db: PgPool,
    pub http: Client,
}
#[instrument(skip_all)]
pub async fn books_handler(State(state): State<AppState>) ->
Json<Vec<Book>> {
    let books =
inventory::list_books(&state.db).await.unwrap_or_default();
    Json(books)
}
#[instrument(skip_all)]
pub async fn order_handler(
    State(state): State<AppState>,
    Json(payload): Json<(i32, Vec<i32>, String)>, // (user_id,
books, card_token)
) -> Result<Json<Order>, StatusCode> {
    let (user_id, book_ids, card_token) = payload;

    // 1. Process payment
    let transaction = payments::process_payment(&state.http,
calculate_total(&state.db, &book_ids).await?, &card_token)
        .await
        .map_err(|_| StatusCode::PAYMENT_REQUIRED)?;

    // 2. Create order record
    let mut order = orders::create_order(&state.db, user_id,
book_ids)
```

```
        .await
        .map_err(|_| StatusCode::INTERNAL_SERVER_ERROR)?;

    // 3. Attach transaction ID (optional field in Order)
    order.transaction_id = Some(transaction);

    Ok(Json(order))
}
```

Here, we injected **AppState** with shared **db** and **http** client. The **order_handler** ran payment first, then created the order. Errors short-circuit with an HTTP status. And the **#[instrument]** covered all steps for traceability.

With this, our server can now process complex workflows end to end, and also able to maintain high performance.

Integrating Third-party APIs

Let us now learn something new wherein we look towards to enrich our app with external services. This we can do by integrating external services with **reqwest**. It will benefit us with real-world APIs to add dynamic book metadata and payment processing. For this, we will define the data models for external responses, then we implement a metadata module for the OpenLibrary API, and expose new HTTP endpoints that our client can consume.

Fetching Metadata from OpenLibrary

Defining Data Model

Within the **src/common/metadata.rs**, we firstly define the structs that can mirror the OpenLibrary JSON:

```
// src/common/metadata.rs
use serde::Deserialize;
#[derive(Deserialize, Debug)]
pub struct AuthorRef {
    pub key: String,
}
```

```
#[derive(Deserialize, Debug)]
pub struct CoverUrls {
    pub small: Option<String>,
    pub medium: Option<String>,
    pub large: Option<String>,
}
#[derive(Deserialize, Debug)]
pub struct BookMetadata {
    pub title: String,
    pub authors: Vec<AuthorRef>,
    pub publish_date: Option<String>,
    #[serde(rename = "cover")]
    pub covers: Option<CoverUrls>,
}
```

These types will allow the Serde to deserialize the JSON returned by the **https://openlibrary.org/isbn/{ISBN}.json**.

Implementing Metadata Module

To implement, we then create **src/server/metadata.rs** and use **reqwest::Client** to fetch and parse the API:

```
// src/server/metadata.rs
use reqwest::Client;
use tracing::instrument;
use common::metadata::BookMetadata;
#[instrument(skip(client, isbn))]
pub async fn fetch_metadata(
    client: &Client,
    isbn: &str,
) -> Result<BookMetadata, reqwest::Error> {
```

```
    let url = format!("https://openlibrary.org/isbn/{}.json",
isbn);
    let resp = client
        .get(&url)
        .send()
        .await?
        .error_for_status()?;        // Returns Err if 4xx/5xx
    let metadata = resp.json::<BookMetadata>().await?;
    Ok(metadata)
}
```

Here, the **#[instrument]** logs the **isbn** parameter and timing. And, the **error_for_status()** converts HTTP errors into Rust errors for unified handling.

Exposing Metadata Endpoint

In **src/server/handlers.rs**, we then wire this into an Axum route:

```
use axum::{extract::Path, Json, State};
use common::metadata::BookMetadata;
use reqwest::Client;
use tracing::instrument;
use crate::metadata::fetch_metadata;
pub struct AppState {
    pub http: Client,
    // ... existing state
}
#[instrument(skip_all)]
pub async fn metadata_handler(
    State(state): State<AppState>,
    Path(isbn): Path<String>,
) -> Result<Json<BookMetadata>, (StatusCode, String)> {
    match fetch_metadata(&state.http, &isbn).await {
```

```
        Ok(data) => Ok(Json(data)),
        Err(e) => {
            tracing::error!(error = %e, isbn, "Failed to fetch
metadata");
            Err((StatusCode::BAD_GATEWAY, "Metadata fetch
failed".into()))
        }
    }
}
```

And then we add the route in **main.rs**:

```
use axum::routing::get;
// inside our Router::new()
    .route("/api/metadata/:isbn", get(metadata_handler))
```

After this, our server now serves **/api/metadata/{isbn}**, returning rich book details straight from OpenLibrary.

Integrating Payment Gateways

You've already implemented a payment module using **reqwest::Client**. So now, we will connect a real gateway by doing the following:

1. **Configure API Keys** in our **/config/.env**.
2. **Reuse the existing process_payment** function in **src/server/payments.rs**, ensuring you pass the **Client** from **AppState**.
3. **Handle webhooks** by adding a POST route **/api/payment/webhook** to verify transaction statuses asynchronously.

Consuming Third-Party Data in Leptos Components

Finally, we then create a Leptos component to display the metadata for which we edit the following in the **src/client/book_metadata.rs**:

```
use leptos::*;
use common::metadata::BookMetadata;
#[component]
```

```
pub fn BookMetadataViewer(cx: Scope, isbn: String) -> Element
{
    let metadata = create_signal(cx, None::<BookMetadata>);
    spawn_local(async move {
        let fetched: BookMetadata =
            reqwest::get(&format!("/api/metadata/{}", isbn))
                .await.unwrap()
                .json().await.unwrap();
        metadata.set(Some(fetched));
    });
    view! { cx,
        {move || if let Some(data) = metadata.get().as_ref() {
            view! { cx,
                <div>
                    <h2>{data.title.clone()}</h2>
                    <p>{format!("Published: {}",
data.publish_date.clone().unwrap_or_default())}</p>
                    {data.covers.as_ref().and_then(|c|
c.medium.clone()).map(|url|
                        view! { cx, <img src=url /> }
                    ).unwrap_or_default()}
                </div>
            }
        } else {
            view! { cx, <p>"Loading metadata..."</p> }
        }}
    }
}
```

This whole process brings dynamic, real-world data into our application, with further demonstrating the leverage of Rust's async ecosystem in our app to deliver a rich user experience.

Securing and Logging Requests

Finally in this chapter, we will now enhance LibroCommerce's server by adding middleware that logs every request and enforces basic JWT-based authentication. We will reuse the **`Tracing`** setup for structured logs and install **`jsonwebtoken`** to verify tokens. This approach ensures that each incoming HTTP request is logged with context and that protected routes require a valid token before proceeding.

Add 'jsonwebtoken'

Let us first add the dependency as following to our **`cargo.toml`**:

```
[dependencies]
jsonwebtoken = "8"
axum = { version = "0.6", features = ["headers"] }
tower-http = { version = "0.3", features = ["trace", "auth"] }
tracing = "0.1"
tracing-subscriber = { version = "0.3", features = ["env-
filter", "fmt", "json"] }
```

Then run the **`cargo update`** to fetch the new crate.

Define JWT Claims and Helper

Create **`src/server/auth.rs`**:

```
// src/server/auth.rs
use jsonwebtoken::{DecodingKey, Validation, decode, Algorithm,
errors::Error};
use serde::{Deserialize, Serialize};
use tracing::instrument;
static SECRET: &[u8] = b"your-256-bit-secret"; // Replace with
env var in production
#[derive(Debug, Serialize, Deserialize)]
pub struct Claims {
    pub sub: String,        // subject (e.g., user ID)
    pub exp: usize,         // expiration as UTC timestamp
```

```
}
#[instrument(skip(token))]
pub fn validate_jwt(token: &str) -> Result<Claims, Error> {
    let mut validation = Validation::new(Algorithm::HS256);
    validation.validate_exp = true;
    let token_data = decode::<Claims>(
        token,
        &DecodingKey::from_secret(SECRET),
        &validation
    )?;
    Ok(token_data.claims)
}
```

Here, the **Claims** struct maps the JWT payload, and the **validate_jwt** decodes and validates expiration.

Implement Authentication Middleware

To implement the authentication middleware, we need to add the following in the **src/server/middleware.rs**:

```
// src/server/middleware.rs
use axum::{
    async_trait,
    extract::RequestParts,
    http::{StatusCode, Request},
    middleware::Next,
    response::Response
};
use tracing::{instrument, error};
use crate::auth::validate_jwt;
#[instrument]
pub async fn auth_middleware<B>(
```

```
    mut req: RequestParts<B>,
    next: Next<B>,
) -> Result<Response, StatusCode> {
    // Extract Authorization header
    let auth_header = if let Some(h) =
req.headers().get("authorization") {
        h.to_str().map_err(|_| StatusCode::BAD_REQUEST)?
    } else {
        return Err(StatusCode::UNAUTHORIZED);
    };
    // Expect "Bearer <token>"
    let token = auth_header
        .strip_prefix("Bearer ")
        .ok_or(StatusCode::UNAUTHORIZED)?;
    // Validate JWT
    match validate_jwt(token) {
        Ok(claims) => {
            tracing::info!(user = %claims.sub, "JWT
validated");
            // Optionally store claims in request extensions:
            req.extensions_mut().insert(claims);
            Ok(next.run(req).await)
        }
        Err(e) => {
            error!(error = %e, "JWT validation failed");
            Err(StatusCode::UNAUTHORIZED)
        }
    }
}
```

Here, the middleware extracts the **Authorization** header, strips **Bearer**, and calls

validate_jwt. On success, it logs the **sub** claim and proceeds; on failure, it returns **401 Unauthorized**.

Apply Middleware to Routes

Next, in our **src/server/main.rs**, we then import and layer the middleware:

```
use axum::{
    routing::{get, post},
    Router,
    middleware::from_fn,
};
use tower_http::trace::TraceLayer;
mod handlers;
mod middleware as mw;
#[tokio::main]
async fn main() {
    // Tracing subscriber setup omitted for brevity...

    let protected_routes = Router::new()
        .route("/api/order", post(handlers::order_handler))
        .route("/api/user/profile",
get(handlers::profile_handler))
        .layer(from_fn(mw::auth_middleware));
    let app = Router::new()
        .route("/", get(handlers::root))
        .route("/api/books", get(handlers::books_handler))
        .route("/api/metadata/:isbn",
get(handlers::metadata_handler))
        // mount protected routes under /api
        .nest("/api", protected_routes)
        // logging layer
```

```
        .layer(TraceLayer::new_for_http());
    let addr = "127.0.0.1:3000".parse().unwrap();
    tracing::info!(%addr, "Server started");
    axum::Server::bind(&addr)
        .serve(app.into_make_service())
        .await
        .unwrap();
}
```

Here, the **from_fn(mw::auth_middleware)** applies authentication only to routes under **/api/order** and **/api/user/profile**. And the **TraceLayer::new_for_http()** logs each request's method, URI, status, and latency.

Testing Authentication and Logging

After this, we then generate a JWT matching our **Claims** and secret:

```
# Example using jwt-cli (install separately)
jwt encode --secret 'your-256-bit-secret' --no-print 'sub:
"1", exp: <future timestamp>'
```

Next, we then test the **Protected Route** without token:

```
curl -i http://localhost:3000/api/order
# Expect HTTP/1.1 401 Unauthorized
```

Then, we try to test it with Token:

```
curl -i -H "Authorization: Bearer <token>" \
    -d '{"user_id":1,"book_ids":[101],"card_token":"tok"}' \
    http://localhost:3000/api/order
# Expect order JSON or relevant status
```

After this, each request logs a JSON or formatted entry showing timestamp, method, URI, status, user claim, and request latency.

By adding this middleware, we infuse structured logging for every HTTP request via **TraceLayer**, and enforced JWT-based authentication on sensitive endpoints using

axum::middleware::from_fn and **jsonwebtoken**. These things strengthen our backend's security posture and diagnostics.

Summary

Basically, you built a responsive server using Tokio and Axum that handled dynamic routes like **/api/books** and **/api/book/:id**, enabling multiple HTTP requests to run at the same time without blocking. With Leptos, you can use server-driven rendering and mount components to deliver both API data and HTML pages from the same runtime. You split up the core business logic into the inventory, orders, and payments modules. You used SQLX for database queries and transactions that listed books, updated stock, and created order records. All of this worked reliably. I noticed you added a metadata module that fetched live book info from OpenLibrary via request. It defined shared data models and wired endpoints to parse JSON into Rust structs.

Next, you integrated payment processing with an external gateway, managed success and error responses, and tracked outcomes. You then used structured logging with the Tracing crate, setting up a global subscriber with JSON formatting and environment filtering, and added Tower's TraceLayer to automatically record spans for each request. You finally got JWT-based authentication working through middleware that extracted tokens, decoded claims with jsonwebtoken, and protected sensitive routes under **/api/order** and **/api/user/profile**. You tested with curl and checked the real-time log output, which showed that every request, error, and authorization event was captured. This lets you figure out what's going on and keep an eye on performance.

CHAPTER 4: DATABASE INTEGRATION AND STATE MANAGEMENT

Overview

Let us start with our new chapter wherein you will begin configuring our environment to load sensitive settings from a **.env** file using **dotenv**, such that database credentials and backup paths stay out of source control. You will then initialize an asynchronous PostgreSQL connection pool with **sqlx**, integrating it into our Tokio runtime and Axum application state. You will then design comprehensive data models for books, users, and orders with Serde, leveraging attributes to handle defaults, renaming, and optional fields. You will implement dynamic CRUD operations in a dedicated module, exposing create, read, update, and delete endpoints that interact with our **PgPool**.

Afterwards, you will automate secure database backups by scripting **pg_dump** and scheduling it with cron, using encrypted output and environment-driven configuration. Finally, you will install **Argon2** and **rand** to implement memory-hard password hashing and verification functions, integrating them into user registration and login flows to protect credentials. These steps will give you hands-on experience in stateful data management, secure configuration, and scalable backend design for a production-ready web application.

Connecting App to PostgreSQL

PostgreSQL has a solid reputation for providing reliable, ACID-compliant data storage, which makes sure that every transaction—whether it's a new order insertion or an inventory update—stays consistent even under concurrent load. PostgreSQL's advanced indexing strategies, like B-trees and GIN for full-text search, let you build responsive catalog queries that give our users a smooth browsing experience and instantly return results. It supports JSON and JSONB fields, so you can store flexible metadata alongside your structured rows. This is great for handling different book attributes or user preferences without having to make a bunch of schema migrations. You can add extensions like PostGIS or pg_trgm later to support geolocation searches or fuzzy title matching. You can count on PostgreSQL's connection pooling, replication, and built-in security features to make sure that LibroCommerce can grow while keeping your users' private data safe and providing great performance.

Managing Configuration with Environment Variables

For secure and flexible deployment, you should never hard-code our database credentials. Instead, we must define a **DATABASE_URL** environment variable that follows the format **postgres://user:password@host:port/database**. For better use, you can place this in a **.env** file at the project root:

```
# .env
```

```
DATABASE_URL=postgres://libro_user:secret@localhost:5432/libro
_commerce
```

Our application will use the **dotenv** crate to load this configuration at startup. Ensure you have called **dotenv::dotenv().ok();** early in our **main** function so that **std::env::var("DATABASE_URL")** retrieves the correct value.

Initializing Asynchronous Connection Pool

We begin with creating a dedicated module for database initialization in **src/server/db.rs**. This module uses **sqlx::postgres::PgPoolOptions** to establish a pool of connections that our application can reuse, avoiding the overhead of opening and closing connections on every request.

Following is a quick code snippet for asynchronous function:

```
// src/server/db.rs
use sqlx::postgres::PgPoolOptions;
use sqlx::PgPool;
use std::env;
use tracing::info;
pub async fn init_db_pool() -> PgPool {
    // Read the DATABASE_URL environment variable
    let database_url = env::var("DATABASE_URL")
        .expect("DATABASE_URL must be set");

    // Configure and establish a connection pool
    let pool = PgPoolOptions::new()
        .max_connections(10)
        .connect(&database_url)
        .await
        .expect("Failed to create database pool");

    info!("Connected to PostgreSQL at {}", database_url);
    pool
```

```
}
```

This asynchronous function reads the connection string, configures up to ten concurrent connections, and returns the fully initialized **PgPool**. By making it **async**, you ensure it integrates seamlessly into our Tokio runtime, blocking no threads during setup.

Wiring Pool into App State

With our pool initialization in place, we then integrate it into our server's shared state so that request handlers can access it through the **State** extractor. So therefore, we then update our **main.rs** with following:

```
// src/server/main.rs
use axum::{Router, middleware::from_fn, extract::State};
use reqwest::Client;
use tokio;
use tracing_subscriber;
mod db;
mod handlers;
mod middleware;
#[derive(Clone)]
pub struct AppState {
    pub db_pool: sqlx::PgPool,
    pub http_client: Client,
}
#[tokio::main]
async fn main() {
    // Load env variables
    dotenv::dotenv().ok();

    // Initialize tracing
    tracing_subscriber::fmt().init();
```

```
    // Initialize database pool and HTTP client
    let db_pool = db::init_db_pool().await;
    let http_client = Client::new();
    let state = AppState { db_pool, http_client };
    // Build application router
    let app = Router::new()
        .route("/api/books",
axum::routing::get(handlers::list_books))
        .layer(from_fn(middleware::auth_middleware))
        .with_state(state.clone());
    // Start server
    let addr = "127.0.0.1:3000".parse().unwrap();
    tracing::info!(%addr, "Starting server");
    axum::Server::bind(&addr)
        .serve(app.into_make_service_with_state(state))
        .await
        .unwrap();
}
```

Here, the **AppState** holds our **PgPool** and a shared **reqwest** client. The router is configured with state, and every handler can extract **State<AppState>** to perform asynchronous database queries reliably.

Using Pool in Handlers

Finally, we then look into how to use the request handler. In **src/server/handlers.rs**, we then implement the **list_books** function:

```
// src/server/handlers.rs
use axum::{extract::State, Json};
use common::models::Book;
use sqlx::Row;
use tracing::instrument;
```

```rust
#[instrument(skip(state))]
pub async fn list_books(
    State(state): State<AppState>
) -> Json<Vec<Book>> {
    let rows = sqlx::query!(
        r#"
        SELECT id, title, author, price
        FROM books
        ORDER BY title
        "#
    )
    .fetch_all(&state.db_pool)
    .await
    .expect("Failed to query books");
    // Map SQLx row types into our Book model
    let books = rows.into_iter().map(|r| Book {
        id: r.id,
        title: r.title,
        author: r.author,
        price: r.price,
    }).collect();
    Json(books)
}
```

This handler uses the shared pool for an asynchronous query, then maps each row into the **`Book`** struct before returning JSON. The **`#[instrument]`** macro logs the function entry and timing automatically.

With all steps implemented as shown, you can thn have a secure, asynchronous connection to PostgreSQL with **`sqlx`**, loaded configuration from environment variables, integrated the connection pool into our application state, and demonstrated how to use it in request handlers.

Designing Data Models

We now move on to leverage Rust's type system alongwith **Serde**'s serialization framework. This will help us to define data models that mirror real-world entities in LibroCommerce. It will help us to create structured, type-safe representations for **Book**, **User**, and **Order**, including optional fields and nested types. The Serde's derives and attributes will let us control the JSON mapping cleanly so as to interchange data between our Rust backend, database layer, and client.

Leveraging Serde for Flexible Serialization

The Serde has already been added to our project (**serde = { version = "1.0", features = ["derive"] }** and **serde_json = "1.0"**). By deriving **Serialize** and **Deserialize** on our structs, you enable automatic conversion between Rust types and JSON.

There are additional attributes such as **#[serde(rename = "...")]**, **#[serde(default)]**, and **#[serde(skip_serializing_if = "Option::is_none")]** which gives us precise control over field names, default values, and optional omission.

Defining Book Model

Here, we first update our previously created **src/common/models.rs** with the following **Book** struct:

```
// src/common/models.rs
use serde::{Deserialize, Serialize};
#[derive(Debug, Serialize, Deserialize)]
pub struct Book {
    pub id: i32,
    pub title: String,
    pub author: String,
    pub price: f64,
    #[serde(default)]
    pub stock: i32,                                 // Defaults
to 0 if missing
    #[serde(skip_serializing_if = "Option::is_none")]
```

```
    pub metadata: Option<BookMetadata>,                      // Optional
nested metadata
}
#[derive(Debug, Serialize, Deserialize)]
pub struct BookMetadata {
    #[serde(rename = "publish_date")]
    pub published: Option<String>,                           // Renamed
field in JSON
    #[serde(default)]
    pub pages: u32,                                          // Default
0 if missing
}
```

Here, the **stock** uses **#[serde(default)]** so that if the database or client omits it, Serde supplies **0**. The **metadata** is optional and will be skipped in JSON if **None**, reducing payload size. And, the **BookMetadata** shows how to rename JSON keys and provide defaults.

Defining User Model

Within the **Book** definitions, we then add **User**:

```
#[derive(Debug, Serialize, Deserialize)]
pub struct User {
    pub id: i32,
    pub username: String,
    #[serde(rename = "email_address")]
    pub email: String,                                       // Maps to
"email_address" in JSON
    #[serde(skip_serializing_if = "Option::is_none")]
    pub address: Option<Address>,                            // Nested
optional struct
}
#[derive(Debug, Serialize, Deserialize)]
pub struct Address {
```

```
    pub street: String,
    pub city: String,
    pub postal_code: String,
    pub country: String,
}
```

Here, we are mapping the **email** field to a different JSON property. And, the **Address** demonstrates nested struct usage and optional embedding.

Defining Order Model with Enums

Finally, we then define an **Order** that references both **User** and **Book** IDs and includes an enum for status:

```
#[derive(Debug, Serialize, Deserialize)]
pub struct Order {
    pub id: i32,
    #[serde(rename = "userId")]
    pub user_id: i32,
    #[serde(rename = "bookIds")]
    pub book_ids: Vec<i32>,
    pub total: f64,
    #[serde(default = "default_status")]
    pub status: OrderStatus,                         // Uses
default function
}
#[derive(Debug, Serialize, Deserialize)]
#[serde(rename_all = "lowercase")]
pub enum OrderStatus {
    Pending,
    Confirmed,
    Shipped,
    Cancelled,
```

```
}
fn default_status() -> OrderStatus {
    OrderStatus::Pending
}
```

Here, the **OrderStatus** enum variants serialize as lowercase strings. The **status** defaults to **Pending** if omitted, via **#[serde(default = "default_status")]**.

Once all the above models are in place, our LibroCommerce becomes well equipped to handle complex data flows, including the reading from the database, enriching with metadata, and serving clients with type-safe, well-structured JSON.

Implementing Dynamic CRUD Operations

Now we will look into building a full Create, Read, Update, and Delete (CRUD) functionality for **Book** entities. It will get us skilled in how to manage dynamic data interactions in LibroCommerce's backend.

Defining New and Update DTOs

First, we begin to create data transfer objects to receive client payloads. So for this, we add the following in the **src/common/models.rs**:

```
use serde::{Deserialize, Serialize};
#[derive(Debug, Deserialize)]
pub struct NewBook {
    pub title: String,
    pub author: String,
    pub price: f64,
    pub stock: i32,
}
#[derive(Debug, Deserialize)]
pub struct UpdateBook {
    pub title: Option<String>,
    pub author: Option<String>,
    pub price: Option<f64>,
```

```
    pub stock: Option<i32>,
}
```

Here, the **NewBook** represents the required fields for creation. And, the **UpdateBook** uses **Option** to allow partial updates.

Implementing CRUD Functions

We then create the **src/server/crud.rs** and implement asynchronous functions that operate on **PgPool**:

```
// src/server/crud.rs
use sqlx::PgPool;
use common::models::{Book, NewBook, UpdateBook};
use tracing::instrument;
use anyhow::Result;
/// Inserts a new book and returns the created record.
#[instrument(skip(pool))]
pub async fn create_book(pool: &PgPool, new: NewBook) ->
Result<Book> {
    let record = sqlx::query_as!(
        Book,
        r#"
        INSERT INTO books (title, author, price, stock)
        VALUES ($1, $2, $3, $4)
        RETURNING id, title, author, price, stock
        "#,
        new.title, new.author, new.price, new.stock
    )
    .fetch_one(pool)
    .await?;
    Ok(record)
}
```

```
/// Retrieves a single book by ID.
#[instrument(skip(pool))]
pub async fn get_book(pool: &PgPool, id: i32) -> Result<Book>
{
    let record = sqlx::query_as!(
        Book,
        r#"
        SELECT id, title, author, price, stock
        FROM books
        WHERE id = $1
        "#,
        id
    )
    .fetch_one(pool)
    .await?;
    Ok(record)
}
/// Updates a book's fields and returns the updated record.
#[instrument(skip(pool))]
pub async fn update_book(pool: &PgPool, id: i32, upd:
UpdateBook) -> Result<Book> {
    // Fetch current values
    let mut book = get_book(pool, id).await?;
    if let Some(title) = upd.title { book.title = title; }
    if let Some(author) = upd.author { book.author = author; }
    if let Some(price) = upd.price { book.price = price; }
    if let Some(stock) = upd.stock { book.stock = stock; }
    let record = sqlx::query_as!(
        Book,
        r#"
```

```
        UPDATE books
        SET title = $2, author = $3, price = $4, stock = $5
        WHERE id = $1
        RETURNING id, title, author, price, stock
        "#,
        id, book.title, book.author, book.price, book.stock
    )
    .fetch_one(pool)
    .await?;
    Ok(record)
}
/// Deletes a book, returning the number of affected rows.
#[instrument(skip(pool))]
pub async fn delete_book(pool: &PgPool, id: i32) ->
Result<u64> {
    let result = sqlx::query!(
        "DELETE FROM books WHERE id = $1",
        id
    )
    .execute(pool)
    .await?;
    Ok(result.rows_affected())
}
```

In the above, each function is **async**, uses **#[instrument]** for tracing, and returns a **Result** to unify error handling.

Exposing CRUD Endpoints

Next, we then add the HTTP handlers in **src/server/handlers.rs** to invoke these functions:

```
// src/server/handlers.rs
```

```
use axum::{extract::{State, Path}, Json, http::StatusCode};
use common::models::{Book, NewBook, UpdateBook};
use sqlx::PgPool;
use tracing::instrument;
use crate::crud::{create_book, get_book as db_get,
update_book, delete_book};
#[instrument(skip_all)]
pub async fn create_book_handler(
    State(state): State<AppState>,
    Json(payload): Json<NewBook>,
) -> Result<Json<Book>, StatusCode> {
    create_book(&state.db_pool, payload)
        .await
        .map(Json)
        .map_err(|_| StatusCode::INTERNAL_SERVER_ERROR)
}
#[instrument(skip_all)]
pub async fn get_book_handler(
    State(state): State<AppState>,
    Path(id): Path<i32>,
) -> Result<Json<Book>, StatusCode> {
    db_get(&state.db_pool, id)
        .await
        .map(Json)
        .map_err(|_| StatusCode::NOT_FOUND)
}
#[instrument(skip_all)]
pub async fn update_book_handler(
    State(state): State<AppState>,
    Path(id): Path<i32>,
```

```
    Json(payload): Json<UpdateBook>,
) -> Result<Json<Book>, StatusCode> {
    update_book(&state.db_pool, id, payload)
        .await
        .map(Json)
        .map_err(|_| StatusCode::INTERNAL_SERVER_ERROR)
}
#[instrument(skip_all)]
pub async fn delete_book_handler(
    State(state): State<AppState>,
    Path(id): Path<i32>,
) -> Result<StatusCode, StatusCode> {
    delete_book(&state.db_pool, id)
        .await
        .map(|rows| if rows > 0 { StatusCode::NO_CONTENT }
else { StatusCode::NOT_FOUND })
        .map_err(|_| StatusCode::INTERNAL_SERVER_ERROR)
}
```

Each of the handler extracts **State<AppState>**, path parameters, or JSON payloads, and returns appropriate HTTP statuses.

Registering Routes

Finally, we then add CRUD routes in **main.rs**:

```
use axum::routing::{get, post, put, delete};
let app = Router::new()
    // Create
    .route("/api/books", post(handlers::create_book_handler))
    // Read all books (existing)
    .route("/api/books", get(handlers::list_books_handler))
    // Read one
```

```
    .route("/api/books/:id", get(handlers::get_book_handler))
    // Update
    .route("/api/books/:id",
put(handlers::update_book_handler))
    // Delete
    .route("/api/books/:id",
delete(handlers::delete_book_handler))
    // ... other routes ...
    .with_state(state.clone())
    .layer(TraceLayer::new_for_http());
```

Verifying CRUD Operations

- Create

```
curl -X POST -H "Content-Type: application/json" \
    -d '{"title":"New
Book","author":"Author","price":19.99,"stock":5}' \
    http://localhost:3000/api/books
```

- Read All

```
curl http://localhost:3000/api/books
```

- Read One

```
curl http://localhost:3000/api/books/1
```

- Update

```
curl -X PUT -H "Content-Type: application/json" \
    -d '{"price":17.99}' \
    http://localhost:3000/api/books/1
```

- Delete

```
curl -X DELETE http://localhost:3000/api/books/1
```

We then observe our server logs to see each operation's span and parameters recorded by Tracing. After all these, we can say that we have successfully implemented full, dynamic CRUD operations, empowering LibroCommerce to handle live data interactions in a scalable, type-safe manner.

Setting up Backups and Encryption

Now to setup the backups and encryption, we need to install and configure **dotenv** to manage environment variables securely and **Argon2** to hash user passwords safely. We will see how to load secrets from a **.env** file, use them for database backups, and implement state-of-the-art password hashing in our registration flow.

Installing Dotenv and Argon2

For this, we first add all these dependencies to our **Cargo.toml** under **[dependencies]**:

```
dotenv = "0.15"                # for loading .env configuration
argon2 = "0.3"                 # for password hashing
rand = "0.8"                   # to generate secure salts
cargo update
```

Managing Configuration Securely

We first **Load the .env file** at program start. In **src/server/main.rs**, add at top (already used for **DATABASE_URL**):

```
# .env
DATABASE_URL=postgres://libro_user:secret@localhost:5432/libro
_commerce
BACKUP_PATH=/var/backups/libro
BACKUP_SCHEDULE="0 2 * * *"     # cron: daily at 2 AM
JWT_SECRET=your-256-bit-secret
use dotenv::dotenv;
use std::env;
#[tokio::main]
async fn main() {
```

```
    dotenv().ok();                              // loads .env
into env vars
    let db_url = env::var("DATABASE_URL")?;
    let backup_path = env::var("BACKUP_PATH")?;
    // ...
}
```

We then use the `env::var` throughout our code to retrieve secrets, preventing credentials from appearing in source control.

Automating Database Backups

With **BACKUP_PATH** and **DATABASE_URL** in **.env**, you can create a simple shell script for daily backups:

```
#!/usr/bin/env bash
set -e
source .env
TIMESTAMP=$(date +"%Y%m%d_%H%M%S")
mkdir -p "$BACKUP_PATH"
pg_dump "$DATABASE_URL" | gzip >
"$BACKUP_PATH/libro_$TIMESTAMP.sql.gz"
```

Then we save this as **scripts/backup.sh**, make executable (**chmod +x**), and schedule via cron:

```
crontab -l > cron.tmp
echo "$BACKUP_SCHEDULE    /path/to/backup.sh" >> cron.tmp
crontab cron.tmp && rm cron.tmp
```

This ensures nightly, encrypted (gzip) backups without exposing passwords in scripts.

Password Hashing with Argon2

Now one must know that to securely store user passwords requires hashing with a memory-hard algorithm. So in **src/server/auth.rs**, we implement the hashing and verification:

```
// src/server/auth.rs
```

```
use argon2::{self, Config};
use rand::Rng;
use tracing::instrument;
/// Hashes a plaintext password, returning salt and hash
concatenated.
#[instrument(skip(password))]
pub fn hash_password(password: &str) -> Result<String,
argon2::Error> {
    let salt: [u8; 16] = rand::thread_rng().gen();
    let config = Config::default();
    let hash = argon2::hash_encoded(password.as_bytes(),
&salt, &config)?;
    Ok(hash)  // hash contains salt & parameters
}
/// Verifies a plaintext password against the stored hash.
#[instrument(skip(password, hash))]
pub fn verify_password(password: &str, hash: &str) ->
Result<bool, argon2::Error> {
    argon2::verify_encoded(hash, password.as_bytes())
}
```

Here, the **hash_encoded** embeds the salt and Argon2 parameters in the returned string. And, the **verify_encoded** parses the string and checks the password.

Integrating Hashing

Next, we then update our user registration logic in **src/server/user_accounts.rs**:

```
use crate::auth::{hash_password};
use sqlx::PgPool;
use common::models::User;
use tracing::instrument;
#[instrument(skip(pool, password))]
pub async fn register_user(
```

```
    pool: &PgPool,
    username: &str,
    email: &str,
    password: &str,
) -> Result<User, sqlx::Error> {
    // 1. Hash the password
    let pw_hash = hash_password(password).expect("Password
hashing failed");
    // 2. Insert user record with hashed password
    let user = sqlx::query_as!(
        User,
        r#"
        INSERT INTO users (username, email, password_hash)
        VALUES ($1, $2, $3)
        RETURNING id, username, email
        "#,
        username,
        email,
        pw_hash
    )
    .fetch_one(pool)
    .await?;
    Ok(user)
}
```

Here, we store only the **hash**, never plaintext, and update our **`users`** table to include a **`password_hash`** column.

Verifying Passwords on Login

In our authentication handler, we use **`verify_password`**:

```
// src/server/handlers.rs
```

```
use crate::auth::verify_password;
use sqlx::PgPool;
use axum::{extract::Json, http::StatusCode};
use common::models::UserLogin; // { username, password }
use tracing::instrument;
#[instrument(skip(pool, credentials))]
pub async fn login_handler(
    State(state): State<AppState>,
    Json(credentials): Json<UserLogin>,
) -> Result<Json<TokenResponse>, StatusCode> {
    let record = sqlx::query!(
        "SELECT id, password_hash FROM users WHERE username =
$1",
        credentials.username
    )
    .fetch_one(&state.db_pool)
    .await
    .map_err(|_| StatusCode::UNAUTHORIZED)?;
    if verify_password(&credentials.password,
&record.password_hash)
        .map_err(|_| StatusCode::INTERNAL_SERVER_ERROR)?
    {
        // Issue JWT token...
        Ok(Json(TokenResponse { token: "jwt".into() }))
    } else {
        Err(StatusCode::UNAUTHORIZED)
    }
}
```

With this, we have installed **dotenv** and **Argon2**, set up secure environment variable management, automated encrypted database backups, and implemented robust password hashing and verification. These measures confirms that our application's sensitive data remains protected at rest and in transit.

Summary

Overall, you were successful in establishing a secured asynchronous connection to PostgreSQL using **sqlx**, loading the database URL from environment variables via **dotenv** and creating a pooled **PgPool** for efficient query handling. You were able to define real-world data models for **Book**, **User**, and **Order** with Serde, using derives and attributes to control JSON field names, defaults, and optional values. You implemented full CRUD operations—**create_book**, **get_book**, **update_book**, and **delete_book**—in a dedicated module, then exposed them through HTTP handlers that parsed path parameters and JSON payloads, returning appropriate status codes. You also automated nightly database backups by scripting **pg_dump** with credentials pulled from **.env** and compressing the output.

Later, for user security, you installed **Argon2** and **rand**, implemented **hash_password** and **verify_password** functions to securely store and validate password hashes, and integrated these into the registration and login handlers. Each of these components was instrumented with Tracing for structured logs, ensuring that operations like pool initialization, model serialization, CRUD actions, and password hashing emitted clear diagnostics. By the end of the chapter, our application was equipped to manage stateful data interactions robustly, maintain data integrity through atomic transactions, secure sensitive information at rest and in transit, and provide a solid foundation for further application development.

Chapter 5: Modern Interactions with REST, GraphQL, and OAuth

Overview

In this chapter, we will start by creating RESTful routes that let clients get full book lists, individual book details, place orders, and get order records. Everything is secured with JWT authentication, of course. We will then layer in GraphQL, defining object types and resolvers that allow clients to request precisely the fields they need in a single query, and we will add an interactive GraphiQL interface for rapid exploration.

Next, we will integrate a full OAuth2 flow using GitHub, handling redirects, token exchanges, and user profile retrieval before issuing our own signed JWTs for API security. To keep our API reliable as it evolves, we will want to refactor our router for in-memory testing, write integration tests that hit our endpoints directly, and configure a GitHub Actions pipeline that spins up a test database, applies migrations, and runs all tests on every code change. As you go through these steps, we will see how to combine REST, GraphQL, OAuth2, and continuous testing to deliver a modern, client-driven, and production-ready web API.

Crafting RESTful Endpoints

Now that you've got a modular Axum server on Tokio, hooked it up to PostgreSQL via sqlx with Serde-defined models, and secured routes with JWT middleware and structured logging, you're all set to show off these features through clear RESTful interfaces. We will write handlers that query and manipulate our **books** and **orders** tables, serialize results into JSON via **Json<T>**, and integrate payment and authentication steps. Here, we will now look at the complete code for book and order endpoints to see how our backend logic becomes accessible to clients.

Exposing Book Resources

To begin with, we start with defining two handlers in **src/server/handlers.rs**. The first handler lists all books, pulling rows from the database, mapping them into our **Book** struct, and returning them as JSON. The second handler extracts an **id** from the URL path, fetches the matching row, and responds with a 404 status if not found:

```
// src/server/handlers.rs
use axum::{extract::{Path, State}, Json, http::StatusCode};
use common::models::Book;
use tracing::instrument;
#[instrument(skip_all)]
pub async fn list_books_handler(
    State(state): State<AppState>
```

```
) -> Json<Vec<Book>> {
    let books = sqlx::query_as!(
        Book,
        "SELECT id, title, author, price, stock FROM books
ORDER BY title"
    )
    .fetch_all(&state.db_pool)
    .await
    .unwrap_or_default();
    Json(books)
}
#[instrument(skip_all)]
pub async fn get_book_handler(
    State(state): State<AppState>,
    Path(id): Path<i32>
) -> Result<Json<Book>, StatusCode> {
    let book = sqlx::query_as!(
        Book,
        "SELECT id, title, author, price, stock FROM books
WHERE id = $1",
        id
    )
    .fetch_one(&state.db_pool)
    .await
    .map_err(|_| StatusCode::NOT_FOUND)?;
    Ok(Json(book))
}
```

These functions leverage the shared **AppState** to access our connection pool, while **#[instrument]** captures each call in our tracing logs for real-time diagnostics.

Implementing Order Endpoints

Next, we then expose the order creation and retrieval. The POST handler at **`/api/orders`** accepts a JSON payload containing **`user_id`**, **`book_ids`**, **`total`**, and **`card_token`**. It processes payment, creates the order record, attaches the transaction ID, and returns the complete **`Order`** struct. The GET handler at **`/api/orders/:id`** fetches an existing order or returns 404:

```
// src/server/handlers.rs (continued)
use axum::extract::Json;
use common::models::{Order, NewOrderPayload};
use tracing::instrument;
#[instrument(skip_all)]
pub async fn create_order_handler(
    State(state): State<AppState>,
    Json(payload): Json<NewOrderPayload>
) -> Result<Json<Order>, StatusCode> {
    let tx_id = payments::process_payment(
        &state.http_client,
        payload.total,
        &payload.card_token
    )
    .await
    .map_err(|_| StatusCode::BAD_GATEWAY)?;

    let mut order = orders::create_order(
        &state.db_pool,
        payload.user_id,
        payload.book_ids
    )
    .await
    .map_err(|_| StatusCode::INTERNAL_SERVER_ERROR)?;
```

```
    order.transaction_id = Some(tx_id);
    Ok(Json(order))
}
#[instrument(skip_all)]
pub async fn get_order_handler(
    State(state): State<AppState>,
    Path(id): Path<i32>
) -> Result<Json<Order>, StatusCode> {
    let order = orders::get_order(&state.db_pool, id)
        .await
        .map_err(|_| StatusCode::NOT_FOUND)?;
    Ok(Json(order))
}
```

These handlers illustrate how our existing payment and order modules integrate directly into the HTTP layer.

Registering Routes in main.rs

Finally, we register these handlers in our application router. In **src/server/main.rs**, we then nest our protected order routes under JWT middleware, while leaving book routes public. We apply the **TraceLayer** top have consistent logging as shown below:

```
// src/server/main.rs
use axum::{routing::{get, post}, Router, middleware::from_fn};
use tower_http::trace::TraceLayer;
let order_routes = Router::new()
    .route("/orders", post(create_order_handler))
    .route("/orders/:id", get(get_order_handler))
    .layer(from_fn(auth_middleware));
let app = Router::new()
    .route("/api/books", get(list_books_handler))
```

```
    .route("/api/books/:id", get(get_book_handler))
    .nest("/api", order_routes)
    .layer(TraceLayer::new_for_http())
    .with_state(state.clone());
```

With this setup, requests to **`/api/books`** and **`/api/books/:id`** are publicly accessible, while **`/api/orders`** and **`/api/orders/:id`** require a valid JWT.

Testing RESTful Interfaces

To verify our work, you can run a series of HTTP requests. For example, retrieving all books:

```
curl http://localhost:3000/api/books
```

Or creating an order with a valid token:

```
curl -X POST \
     -H "Authorization: Bearer <token>" \
     -H "Content-Type: application/json" \
     -d
'{"user_id":1,"book_ids":[1,2],"total":29.98,"card_token":"tes
t"}' \
     http://localhost:3000/api/orders
```

In our console, you can see structured logs-complete with timestamps, ranges, and parameters-that confirm each handler is instrumented and our API is fully functional.

Extending API Flexibility

Now knowing that the RESTful endpoints are well crafted for book listings and order operations, you're now ready to layer in GraphQL to give clients the power to request exactly the data they need in a single call. So here, we will integrate the **`async-graphql`** alongside our existing Axum router in order to have a schema that mirrors our **`Book`**, **`User`**, and **`Order`** models, write resolvers that tap into our sqlx-backed business logic, and mount both a GraphQL endpoint and a built-in GraphiQL interface. This lets the clients fetch nested data—such as a user's order history and each order's book detail in one round trip.

Defining GraphQL Types and Schema

To start with, we add the following to our **Cargo.toml**:

```
async-graphql = "4"
async-graphql-axum = "4"
```

Next, in a new module **src/server/graphql.rs**, we map our existing models into GraphQL object types. For this, we use **#[derive(SimpleObject)]** on lightweight types that mirror our Serde models:

```
// src/server/graphql.rs
use async_graphql::{Context, Object, SimpleObject, Schema,
EmptySubscription};
use common::models::{Book, Order};
use sqlx::PgPool;
#[derive(SimpleObject)]
pub struct GqlBook {
    pub id: i32,
    pub title: String,
    pub author: String,
    pub price: f64,
    pub stock: i32,
}
#[derive(SimpleObject)]
pub struct GqlOrder {
    pub id: i32,
    pub user_id: i32,
    pub book_ids: Vec<i32>,
    pub total: f64,
    pub transaction_id: Option<String>,
}
pub struct QueryRoot;
#[Object]
```

```
impl QueryRoot {
    async fn books(&self, ctx: &Context<'_>) ->
async_graphql::Result<Vec<GqlBook>> {
        let pool = ctx.data_unchecked::<PgPool>();
        let rows = sqlx::query_as!(
            Book,
            "SELECT id, title, author, price, stock FROM books
ORDER BY title"
        )
        .fetch_all(pool)
        .await?;
        Ok(rows.into_iter().map(|b| GqlBook {
            id: b.id, title: b.title, author: b.author, price:
b.price, stock: b.stock
        }).collect())
    }
    async fn book(&self, ctx: &Context<'_>, id: i32) ->
async_graphql::Result<GqlBook> {
        let pool = ctx.data_unchecked::<PgPool>();
        let b = sqlx::query_as!(
            Book,
            "SELECT id, title, author, price, stock FROM books
WHERE id = $1",
            id
        )
        .fetch_one(pool)
        .await?;
        Ok(GqlBook { id: b.id, title: b.title, author:
b.author, price: b.price, stock: b.stock })
    }
```

```
    async fn order(&self, ctx: &Context<'_>, id: i32) ->
async_graphql::Result<GqlOrder> {
        let pool = ctx.data_unchecked::<PgPool>();
        let o = sqlx::query_as!(
            Order,
            "SELECT id, user_id, book_ids, total,
transaction_id FROM orders WHERE id = $1",
            id
        )
        .fetch_one(pool)
        .await?;
        Ok(GqlOrder {
            id: o.id, user_id: o.user_id, book_ids:
o.book_ids, total: o.total, transaction_id: o.transaction_id
        })
    }
}
pub type AppSchema = Schema<QueryRoot, EmptyMutation,
EmptySubscription>;
/// Builds the GraphQL schema with shared data.
pub fn create_schema(pool: PgPool) -> AppSchema {
    Schema::build(QueryRoot, EmptyMutation, EmptySubscription)
        .data(pool)
        .finish()
}
```

Here, the **`QueryRoot`** provides methods that fetch data via our sqlx-driven models, then convert into GraphQL objects.

Mounting GraphQL and GraphiQL Endpoints

After constructing the **`AppState`**, call **`create_schema(state.db_pool.clone())`**. Then we extend our router to include both the **`/graphql`** POST endpoint and an interactive

GraphiQL interface at **/graphiql**:

```
// src/server/main.rs
use async_graphql_axum::{GraphQLRequest, GraphQLResponse,
GraphQLSubscription};
use axum::{routing::get, routing::post};
use crate::graphql::{create_schema, AppSchema};
let schema = create_schema(state.db_pool.clone());
let app = Router::new()
    // existing REST routes...
    .route("/graphql", post(|schema: Extension<AppSchema>,
req: GraphQLRequest| async move {

GraphQLResponse(schema.execute(req.into_inner()).await)
    }))
    .route("/graphiql", get(|_| async {
        Html(async_graphql::http::playground_source(

async_graphql::http::GraphQLPlaygroundConfig::new("/graphql"),
        ))
    }))
    .layer(Extension(schema))
    .with_state(state.clone())
    .layer(TraceLayer::new_for_http());
```

This layering the **Extension(schema)** confirms that each handler can access the GraphQL schema. The GraphiQL route returns HTML that lets you experiment with queries right in our browser.

Testing GraphQL Queries

Next, we restart our server and navigate to **http://localhost:3000/graphiql** wherein you can run a query like:

```
query {
```

```
  books {
    id
    title
    author
  }
  book(id: 1) {
    title
    stock
  }
}
```

This single call returns exactly the requested fields for multiple resources, showcasing the flexibility GraphQL adds to our API.

Implementing OAuth and Token-Based Authentication

So, we've got our JWT middleware and basic token authentication down. Now, you'll be adding a full OAuth2 login flow, using GitHub as an example. Then, we'll issue our own Jsonwebtoken to secure the rest of the API calls.

Configuring OAuth2 with Environment Variables

We begin with the Rust OAuth2 crate installation and then adding our OAuth credentials to the **.env** file alongside our existing secrets:

```
# Cargo.toml
oauth2 = { version = "4", features = ["reqwest"] }
serde = { version = "1.0", features = ["derive"] }
```

In our **.env**:

```
GITHUB_CLIENT_ID=your_github_client_id
GITHUB_CLIENT_SECRET=your_github_client_secret
GITHUB_REDIRECT_URL=http://localhost:3000/auth/github/callback
```

```
JWT_SECRET=your-256-bit-secret
```

This keeps our client ID and secret out of source control. Our code will read these values with **dotenv::dotenv().ok()** and **env::var**.

Setting up OAuth2 Client

Within the **src/server/auth_oauth.rs**, we then configure the GitHub OAuth2 client using the **oauth2** crate. Then, we create an **AuthUrl**, **TokenUrl**, and a **RedirectUrl**, and then build a **BasicClient** that we will reuse for both redirect and callback handlers:

```
use oauth2::{
    basic::BasicClient, AuthUrl, ClientId, ClientSecret,
RedirectUrl, Scope, TokenUrl,
};
use std::env;
pub fn oauth_client() -> BasicClient {
    let client_id =
ClientId::new(env::var("GITHUB_CLIENT_ID").unwrap());
    let client_secret =
ClientSecret::new(env::var("GITHUB_CLIENT_SECRET").unwrap());
    let auth_url =
AuthUrl::new("https://github.com/login/oauth/authorize".to_str
ing()).unwrap();
    let token_url =
TokenUrl::new("https://github.com/login/oauth/access_token".to
_string()).unwrap();
    let redirect_url =
RedirectUrl::new(env::var("GITHUB_REDIRECT_URL").unwrap()).unw
rap();
    BasicClient::new(client_id, Some(client_secret), auth_url,
Some(token_url))
        .set_redirect_uri(redirect_url)
}
```

This constructs and returns a client that knows how to start and complete the OAuth flow.

Redirecting Users to GitHub Login

Later, we then expose a GET handler at **/auth/github** that sends the user's browser to GitHub's authorization page. To do this, we make the following edits in the **src/server/handlers.rs**:

```
use axum::{response::Redirect};
use oauth2::CsrfToken;
use crate::auth_oauth::oauth_client;
pub async fn github_auth_redirect() -> Redirect {
    let (authorize_url, _csrf_token) = oauth_client()
        .authorize_url(CsrfToken::new_random)
        .add_scope(Scope::new("read:user".to_string()))
        .url();
    Redirect::to(authorize_url.as_ref())
}
```

This handler builds an authorization URL with a random CSRF token (which you could store in a session or cookie) and then issues an HTTP 302 redirect. The user then logs into GitHub and consents to share their profile.

Handling OAuth Callback

After the user authorizes, GitHub redirects back to **/auth/github/callback?code=...&state=...**. We then implement a POST or GET handler that exchanges the authorization code for an access token, fetches the user's GitHub profile, and finally issues our own JWT:

```
use axum::{extract::Query, response::IntoResponse, Json};
use oauth2::TokenResponse;
use reqwest::Client;
use serde::Deserialize;
use jsonwebtoken::{encode, Header, EncodingKey};
use chrono::{Utc, Duration};
use crate::auth_oauth::oauth_client;
use common::models::User;
```

```
#[derive(Deserialize)]
pub struct AuthRequest {
    code: String,
    state: String,
}
#[derive(Deserialize)]
struct GitHubUser {
    login: String,
    id: u64,
    email: Option<String>,
}
pub async fn github_auth_callback(
    Query(params): Query<AuthRequest>,
) -> impl IntoResponse {
    let token_result = oauth_client()
        .exchange_code(params.code.into())
        .request_async(async_http_client)
        .await;
    if let Ok(token) = token_result {
        let access_token = token.access_token().secret();
        let client = Client::new();
        let user: GitHubUser = client
            .get("https://api.github.com/user")
            .bearer_auth(access_token)
            .header("User-Agent", "librocommerce")
            .send()
            .await
            .unwrap()
            .json()
```

```
            .await
            .unwrap();
        // Here you would create or fetch a local user record
in our database.
        let local_user = User {
            id: user.id as i32,
            username: user.login.clone(),
            email: user.email.clone().unwrap_or_default(),
        };
        // Now generate a JWT for our own API
        #[derive(serde::Serialize)]
        struct Claims {
            sub: String,
            exp: usize,
        }
        let expiration = Utc::now()
            .checked_add_signed(Duration::hours(24))
            .expect("valid timestamp")
            .timestamp() as usize;
        let claims = Claims {
            sub: local_user.id.to_string(),
            exp: expiration,
        };
        let jwt = encode(
            &Header::default(),
            &claims,

&EncodingKey::from_secret(env::var("JWT_SECRET").unwrap().as_r
ef()),
        ).unwrap();
```

```
        // Return the JWT to the client; you could also set a
cookie here.
        Json(serde_json::json!({ "token": jwt }))
    } else {
        (axum::http::StatusCode::UNAUTHORIZED, "OAuth
failed".into())
    }
}
```

What this handler does is show a real-world scenario. You can use a third-party login, map the external user into our domain, and then make a signed token that our own middleware can validate for later requests.

Through these steps, you have infused our application with advanced authentication, enabling secure, flexible login via GitHub and seamless authorization for every protected route in LibroCommerce.

Automated API Testing

We've already built a modular Axum server with REST and GraphQL endpoints, connected it to PostgreSQL via sqlx, implemented business logic for books and orders, integrated OAuth and JWT authentication, and added structured logging. Now we'll go ahead and codify our API expectations as integration tests that run automatically on every code change, making sure our endpoints work correctly under continuous integration.

Refactoring to Expose Router

So, to do this, we first extract our router construction into a reusable function so tests can spin up the same server instance in memory. Here, we create a new file **`src/server/app.rs`**:

```
// src/server/app.rs
use axum::{Router, middleware::from_fn};
use tower_http::trace::TraceLayer;
use crate::{
    handlers::{list_books_handler, get_book_handler,
create_order_handler, get_order_handler},
    middleware::auth_middleware,
    db::init_db_pool,
```

```
    auth_oauth::oauth_client,
    graphql::create_schema,
};
use reqwest::Client;
use sqlx::PgPool;
pub struct AppState {
    pub db_pool: PgPool,
    pub http_client: Client,
    pub gql_schema: AppSchema,
}
pub async fn create_app() -> Router {
    dotenv::dotenv().ok();
    let db_pool = init_db_pool().await;
    let http_client = Client::new();
    let gql_schema = create_schema(db_pool.clone());
    let state = AppState { db_pool, http_client, gql_schema };

    Router::new()
        .route("/api/books",
axum::routing::get(list_books_handler))
        .route("/api/books/:id",
axum::routing::get(get_book_handler))
        .route("/api/orders",
axum::routing::post(create_order_handler))
        .route("/api/orders/:id",
axum::routing::get(get_order_handler))
        .route("/graphql",
axum::routing::post(async_graphql_axum::GraphQLRequest::execut
e))
        .route("/graphiql", axum::routing::get(|| async {
            axum::response::Html(
```

```
                async_graphql::http::playground_source(

async_graphql::http::GraphQLPlaygroundConfig::new("/graphql"),
                )
            )
        }))

.layer(from_fn(auth_middleware).with_state(state.clone()))
        .layer(TraceLayer::new_for_http())
        .with_state(state)
}
```

In our **main.rs**, we then call **create_app().await** and bind it to a socket.

Writing Integration Tests

Now, under the **tests** directory, we then create **tests/api_tests.rs** and these tests start the in-memory router and send HTTP requests directly, without binding to a network port:

```
// tests/api_tests.rs
use axum::body::Body;
use axum::http::{Request, StatusCode};
use tower::ServiceExt; // for `oneshot`
use serde_json::json;
use librocommerce_server::create_app; // adjust import path
#[tokio::test]
async fn test_list_books() {
    let app = create_app().await;
    let response = app
        .oneshot(
            Request::builder()
                .uri("/api/books")
                .body(Body::empty())
```

```
                .unwrap(),
        )
        .await
        .unwrap();
    assert_eq!(response.status(), StatusCode::OK);
    let body =
hyper::body::to_bytes(response.into_body()).await.unwrap();
    let books: Vec<serde_json::Value> =
serde_json::from_slice(&body).unwrap();
    // At least return an array (could be empty in fresh DB)
    assert!(books.is_array());
}
#[tokio::test]
async fn test_create_and_get_book() {
    let app = create_app().await;
    // Create a new book
    let payload = json!({
        "title": "Test Driven Development",
        "author": "Kent Beck",
        "price": 29.99,
        "stock": 10
    });
    let req = Request::builder()
        .method("POST")
        .uri("/api/books")
        .header("content-type", "application/json")
        .body(Body::from(payload.to_string()))
        .unwrap();
    let resp = app.clone().oneshot(req).await.unwrap();
    assert_eq!(resp.status(), StatusCode::OK);
```

```
    let body =
hyper::body::to_bytes(resp.into_body()).await.unwrap();
    let created: serde_json::Value =
serde_json::from_slice(&body).unwrap();
    let id = created.get("id").unwrap().as_i64().unwrap();
    // Retrieve the same book
    let req = Request::builder()
        .uri(format!("/api/books/{}", id))
        .body(Body::empty())
        .unwrap();
    let resp = app.oneshot(req).await.unwrap();
    assert_eq!(resp.status(), StatusCode::OK);
    let body =
hyper::body::to_bytes(resp.into_body()).await.unwrap();
    let fetched: serde_json::Value =
serde_json::from_slice(&body).unwrap();
    assert_eq!(fetched.get("title").unwrap(), "Test Driven
Development");
}
```

All these tests demonstrate to programmatically exercise our API, validate status codes, and inspect response bodies. If we want, we may add similar tests for order endpoints, GraphQL queries, and OAuth callback flows.

Configuring GitHub Actions for Continuous API Testing

And lastly, if we think its important, then we can automate these tests in our CI pipeline. To make it happen we simply include the following in **github/workflows/ci.yml**:

```
name: CI
on: [push, pull_request]
jobs:
  test:
    runs-on: ubuntu-latest
    steps:
```

```
      - uses: actions/checkout@v2

      - name: Install Rust
        uses: actions-rs/toolchain@v1
        with:
          toolchain: stable
          override: true
      - name: Set up PostgreSQL
        uses: Harmon758/postgresql-action@v1.0.0
        with:
          postgresql version: "13"
          packages: "postgresql-contrib"
      - name: Run Database Migrations
        run: diesel migration run # or our chosen migration
tool
      - name: Run Unit and Integration Tests
        run: cargo test -- --test-threads=1
```

The above workflow checks out our code, installs Rust, spins up PostgreSQL, applies migrations, and executes both unit tests and the integration tests in **`tests/api_tests.rs`**. The **`--test-threads=1`** flag serializes tests when they depend on a shared database. With this setup, every push or pull request will validate that our REST and GraphQL endpoints, authentication flows, and database interactions continue to work as you evolve the codebase—providing rapid feedback and safeguarding the reliability of our API.

Summary

To sum up, you successfully defined the clear RESTful handlers for our book and order resources, with the help of Axum's extractors, JSON payloads, and sqlx. You explored the GraphQL via the async-graphql crate, created a schema that mirrored our existing **`Book`** and **`Order`** models, and mounted both a **`/graphql`** endpoint and an interactive GraphiQL playground, giving clients fine-grained control over the data they fetched.

Next, referring to JWT middleware, you implemented an OAuth2 login flow with GitHub using the oauth2 crate, exchanged authorization codes for access tokens, retrieved a GitHub user profile, and issued our own JWT for securing subsequent requests. To achieve reliability, you refactored our router into a reusable **create_app** function, wrote integration tests that exercised our REST and GraphQL endpoints in memory, and validated HTTP status codes and response bodies. Finally, you automated these tests in a GitHub Actions workflow that spins up PostgreSQL, applies migrations, and runs both unit and integration tests on every push or pull request. By the end, our API surface was robust, flexible, secure, and continuously validated, equipping you to build seamless client–server interactions in a production-grade environment.

Chapter 6: Front-end Development with Leptos and WebAssembly

Overview

In this chapter, we will begin with integrating WebAssembly into our Leptos workflow. We will add the **wasm32-unknown-unknown** target, install **wasm-bindgen-cli**, and build our client-side Rust code into a WebAssembly module with JavaScript glue code. You will then update our HTML to load and initialize the **.wasm** bundle, giving our application near-native performance in the browser.

Next, you will use VS Code to create a **HomePage** component that fetches book data from our REST API, applies a responsive CSS grid layout, and renders each item in a polished card design. You will extract these UI pieces into modular Leptos components—such as **Card**, **Button**, and **SearchForm**—defining clear props for reuse and maintaining consistent styling across our app. After that, you will implement state management with Leptos signals, initializing a signal to hold our book list, fetching data asynchronously, and triggering automatic re-renders. Finally, you will set up a WebSocket connection to receive live stock updates from the server, parse incoming messages into structured updates, and mutate our signals so that the UI reflects inventory changes in real time.

Compiling to WebAssembly

Since we already learned so far to build a rich backend with Leptos components in our **src/client** directory, we now turn those client-side Rust modules into WebAssembly. The WebAssembly basically lets us run Rust code alongside JavaScript, giving our LibroCommerce frontend faster execution, smaller payloads, and stronger type safety than traditional transpiled languages. The compilation of our Leptos components to a **.wasm** module confirms that the UI updates, state management, and event handling happen at top speed while reusing the same Rust code you wrote for the server.

One must also understand that the WebAssembly compiles directly to a compact binary format that modern browsers execute at near-native speed. In the context of Leptos, that means our reactive components — with their fine-grained updates and efficient diffing — run without the overhead of a JavaScript runtime. Our LibroCommerce UI, from rendering book lists to managing complex shopping-cart state, benefits from predictable performance, reduced garbage-collection pauses, and the ability to leverage Rust's concurrency model in future releases. Now here, the security aspect is also enhanced, as the WebAssembly sandbox isolates our code from the rest of the page. By shipping lean **.wasm** bundles, you lower download sizes and improve initial load times, giving our users a snappier experience as they browse and interact with our application.

Setting up WebAssembly Toolchain

To compile our client code, first add the WebAssembly target and install the binding tool. In our Linux terminal, run:

```
rustup target add wasm32-unknown-unknown
cargo install wasm-bindgen-cli
```

The first command instructs Rust to support WebAssembly as a compilation target. The second installs the **wasm-bindgen** CLI, which generates the JavaScript glue code to load and interact with our **.wasm** module in the browser.

Building Leptos Components

With the toolchain in place, we then navigate to our project root and issue a release-mode build targeting WebAssembly:

```
cargo build --release --target wasm32-unknown-unknown
```

This produces a **.wasm** file at **target/wasm32-unknown-unknown/release/libro_commerce.wasm** (where **libro_commerce** matches our crate name).

We then generate the JavaScript bindings:

```
wasm-bindgen \
  --out-dir static/pkg \
  --target web \
  target/wasm32-unknown-unknown/release/libro_commerce.wasm
```

The **static/pkg** folder now contains **libro_commerce.js** and **libro_commerce_bg.wasm**, ready for the browser.

Loading WebAssembly Module in HTML

Next, we then update our **static/index.html** to import and initialize the generated code:

```
<!DOCTYPE html>
<html lang="en">
<head>
  <meta charset="UTF-8" />
  <title>LibroCommerce</title>
</head>
<body>
```

```
  <div id="root"></div>
  <script type="module">
    import init, { start } from "./pkg/libro_commerce.js";
    async function run() {
      await init();
      start(); // Leptos entrypoint, mounts our root component
    }
    run();
  </script>
</body>
</html>
```

Here, the **init()** loads the **.wasm** module, and **start()** is the function you defined with **#[wasm_bindgen(start)]** in our **lib.rs**, which mounts our Leptos root component into the **#root** element.

Verifying WebAssembly Frontend

And lastly, we then serve the **static** directory using a simple server:

```
python3 -m http.server 8080 --directory static
```

With this, our frontend is now running on WebAssembly, ready to deliver high-performance, interactive experiences as we continue to build out our app.

Building Responsive Home Page

We now look into creating a dynamic, responsive home page that fetches our catalog via REST and displays each book in a modern grid layout. So here, we will add a **HomePage** component, fetch data with **reqwest**, and apply simple responsive styles so our book cards adapt across screen sizes.

Setting up HomePage Component

To start with, we at first expand the **src/client** folder in the Explorer pane and create a new file named **home_page.rs**. This file will export a **HomePage** component that Leptos can mount. In our **src/client/lib.rs**, add **mod home_page;** at the top so our new module is included in the build.

```
// src/client/lib.rs
mod hello;
mod home_page; // add this line
use leptos::*;
use hello::HelloWorld;
use home_page::HomePage;
#[wasm_bindgen(start)]
pub fn start() {
    mount_to_body(|cx| view! { cx,
        <div>
            <HomePage/>
        </div>
    });
}
```

Then save both files.

Fetching Book Data from REST Endpoint

In **home_page.rs**, we then define our component in which we will create a **books** signal, then spawn an asynchronous task to fetch **/api/books**:

```
// src/client/home_page.rs
use leptos::*;
use common::models::Book;
#[component]
pub fn HomePage(cx: Scope) -> Element {
    // Signal to store list of books
    let books = create_signal(cx, Vec::<Book>::new());
    // Fetch books on mount
    spawn_local(async move {
```

```
        let fetched: Vec<Book> = reqwest::get("/api/books")
            .await.unwrap()
            .json().await.unwrap();
        books.set(fetched);
    });
    view! { cx,
        <main class="container">
            <h1 class="title">"Welcome to LibroCommerce"</h1>
            <div class="grid">
                {books.get().iter().map(|book| {
                    let title = book.title.clone();
                    let author = book.author.clone();
                    let price = book.price;
                    view! { cx,
                        <div class="card">
                            <h2 class="card-
title">{title}</h2>
                            <p class="card-
author">{format!("by {}", author)}</p>
                            <p class="card-
price">{format!("${:.2}", price)}</p>
                        </div>
                    }
                }).collect::<Vec<_>>()}
            </div>
        </main>
    }
}
```

This will use **reqwest** to call our REST endpoint and updates the **books** signal once the JSON is parsed. And the Leptos then re-renders the grid with one card per book.

Implementing Responsive Grid Layout

Now here, if we want to make the cards adapt to different screen sizes, we can do it by simply adding a CSS file in our **static** directory i.e. **static/styles.css** and include the respective responsive styles as shown in the following:

```
/* static/styles.css */
.container {
  max-width: 1200px;
  margin: 0 auto;
  padding: 1rem;
}
.title {
  text-align: center;
  font-size: 2rem;
  margin-bottom: 1rem;
}
.grid {
  display: grid;
  gap: 1rem;
  grid-template-columns: repeat(auto-fit, minmax(200px, 1fr));
}
.card {
  background: #fff;
  border-radius: 0.5rem;
  padding: 1rem;
  box-shadow: 0 2px 4px rgba(0,0,0,0.1);
}
.card-title {
  margin: 0;
  font-size: 1.25rem;
```

```
}
.card-author,
.card-price {
  margin: 0.25rem 0;
  color: #555;
}
```

Then reference this CSS in our **static/index.html** head:

```
<link rel="stylesheet" href="styles.css" />
```

If you refresh the page, you'll see a responsive grid: on desktop, multiple columns; on mobile, a single column.

Integrating HomePage into App

With our component and styles in place, we then rebuild our WebAssembly bundle:

```
cargo build --release --target wasm32-unknown-unknown
wasm-bindgen --out-dir static/pkg --target web target/wasm32-unknown-unknown/release/libro_commerce.wasm
```

And then we run our static server:

```
python3 -m http.server 8080 --directory static
```

After this, you should now see a polished home page titled "Welcome to LibroCommerce," with book cards laid out in a responsive grid, and each card displays the title, author, and price fetched from our REST API.

Crafting Modular Components

After assembling our responsive home page, we will now extract its elements into reusable Leptos components—cards, buttons, and forms—that can be shared across our application. So here we will try to create a **components** folder and define each UI piece with clear inputs (props).

Creating Card Component

Create a new directory named **components** within **src/client**. Inside it, add **card.rs**. In this file, we define a **Card** component that accepts **title**, **subtitle**, and **price** as properties:

```
// src/client/components/card.rs
use leptos::*;
#[component]
pub fn Card(
    cx: Scope,
    #[prop(into)] title: String,
    #[prop(into)] subtitle: String,
    price: f64,
) -> Element {
    view! { cx,
        <div class="card">
            <h2 class="card-title">{title}</h2>
            <p class="card-subtitle">{subtitle}</p>
            <p class="card-price">{format!("${:.2}",
price)}</p>
        </div>
    }
}
```

Here, the **`#[prop(into)]`** allows callers to pass **`&str`** or **`String`**, and **`price`** is a plain **`f64`**. And replace each inline **`<div class="card">`**...**`</div>`** with our new **`Card`** component:

```
use components::card::Card;
// …
view! { cx,
    <main class="container">
        <h1 class="title">"Welcome to LibroCommerce"</h1>
        <div class="grid">
            {books.get().iter().map(|book| {
```

```
                view! { cx,
                    <Card
                        title=book.title.clone()
                        subtitle=format!("by {}", book.author)
                        price=book.price
                    />
                }
            }).collect::<Vec<_>>()}
        </div>
    </main>
}
```

The Rust Analyzer will instantly pick up the new import; you then use **`Ctrl+.`** to auto-import if needed. Now every book card is rendered by a single component, ensuring any style change to **`.card`** applies universally.

Building Button Component

The Buttons appear throughout our UI—on order forms, navigation, or modal dialogs. We can create **`button.rs`** in the **`components`** folder:

```
// src/client/components/button.rs
use leptos::*;
#[component]
pub fn Button(
    cx: Scope,
    #[prop(into)] label: String,
    on_click: EventHandler<MouseEvent>,
) -> Element {
    view! { cx,
        <button class="btn" on:click=on_click>
            {label}
        </button>
```

```
    }
}
```

The **on_click** prop uses Leptos' **EventHandler**, so you pass closures from parent components. We can add styling in **styles.css**:

```
.btn {
    background-color: #0070f3;
    color: white;
    padding: 0.5rem 1rem;
    border: none;
    border-radius: 0.25rem;
    cursor: pointer;
}
.btn:hover {
    background-color: #005bb5;
}
```

To add more buttons, such as in our order form—you simply write:

```
use components::button::Button;
// …
view! { cx,
    <Button label="Add to Cart" on_click=move |_|
handle_add_to_cart() />
}
```

This makes our buttons visually consistent and behaviorally predictable.

Implementing Search Form Component

The search form often reappears on multiple pages. We can define the **search_form.rs** as below:

```
// src/client/components/search_form.rs
use leptos::*;
```

```
#[component]
pub fn SearchForm(
    cx: Scope,
    placeholder: String,
    on_search: EventHandler<FocusEvent>,
) -> Element {
    view! { cx,
        <form on:submit=move |ev| {
            ev.prevent_default();
            on_search.call(ev);
        }>
            <input
                class="search-input"
                type="text"
                placeholder=placeholder
                name="query"
            />
            <button class="btn"
type="submit">"Search"</button>
        </form>
    }
}
```

Then include the styles:

```
.search-input {
    padding: 0.5rem;
    border: 1px solid #ccc;
    border-radius: 0.25rem;
    margin-right: 0.5rem;
    width: 200px;
```

```
}
```

You can then add a search bar to **HomePage**:

```
use components::search_form::SearchForm;
// …
let query = create_signal(cx, "".to_string());
let handle_search = move |ev| {
    if let Some(input) =
ev.target().unchecked_into::<web_sys::HtmlInputElement>().valu
e().as_ref().into() {
        query.set(input.clone());
        // trigger filtering or fetch new API call…
    }
};
view! { cx,
    <div class="search-container">
        <SearchForm
            placeholder="Search books..."
            on_search=handle_search
        />
    </div>
}
```

This single **SearchForm** component can be reused wherever you need a search bar, and its logic is encapsulated cleanly.

With **Card**, **Button**, and **SearchForm** defined, you avoid rewriting markup or handlers in multiple places. For instance, in a future admin dashboard you might list pending orders using a similar card layout, or use **Button** for "Confirm Order" actions. By extracting UI elements into modular components, you achieve a clean separation of concerns, consistent styling, and maintainability. Each component can now evolve independently—update the **.card** style once, and every **Card** across LibroCommerce reflects the change immediately.

Managing Client-State and Real-Time Synchronization

Once our components are compiled to WebAssembly and you've crafted a responsive home page with reusable **Card**, **Button**, and **SearchForm** components, the next step is ensuring our UI stays synchronized with backend changes in real time. So here, we will explore how we could store application state in signals, subscribe to a WebSocket feed of stock updates, and automatically re-render our book cards whenever the server broadcasts changes.

Leveraging Leptos Signals

At the heart of Leptos' reactivity model are signals—lightweight, observable value holders. When you created our **HomePage** component, you used **create_signal(cx, Vec::<Book>::new())** to hold the list of books. Whenever you called **books.set(new_list)** or mutated via **books.update(...)**, Leptos detected the change and re-rendered any affected portions of the UI. Signals give you a simple API:

```
let books = create_signal(cx, Vec::<Book>::new());
// update entire list
books.set(fetched_books);
// update inline
books.update(|list| {
    if let Some(book) = list.iter_mut().find(|b| b.id ==
update.id) {
        book.stock = update.stock;
    }
});
```

If you put all your book list info in one signal, you can update it in real time without messing with the individual components.

Integrating WebSockets

To push live stock changes, we will expose a WebSocket endpoint on our server, say at **ws://localhost:3000/ws/stock_updates**. On the client, you open a connection and attach an event listener that parses JSON messages and updates our **books** signal accordingly.

In **home_page.rs**, after our initial data fetch, we add the following block:

```
use wasm_bindgen::JsCast;
use web_sys::MessageEvent;
use serde::Deserialize;
// Define the shape of incoming stock updates
#[derive(Deserialize)]
struct StockUpdate {
    id: i32,
    stock: i32,
}
spawn_local(async move {
    // Open WebSocket connection
    let ws =
web_sys::WebSocket::new("ws://localhost:3000/ws/stock_updates"
)
        .expect("Failed to open WebSocket");
    ws.set_binary_type(web_sys::BinaryType::Arraybuffer);
    // Clone the books signal for the closure
    let books_clone = books.clone();
    // Create a JS closure to handle incoming messages
    let onmessage = Closure::wrap(Box::new(move |event:
MessageEvent| {
        if let Ok(txt) = event.data().as_string() {
            if let Ok(update) =
serde_json::from_str::<StockUpdate>(&txt) {
                books_clone.update(|list| {
                    if let Some(book) =
list.iter_mut().find(|b| b.id == update.id) {
                        book.stock = update.stock;
                    }
                });
```

```
            }
        }
    }) as Box<dyn FnMut(_)>);

ws.set_onmessage(Some(onmessage.as_ref().unchecked_ref()));
    onmessage.forget();
});
```

This code runs alongside our initial REST fetch. Each time the server pushes **{"id": 3, "stock": 5}**, the corresponding book in our **books** vector is updated, and Leptos re-renders its **Card** component to show the new stock count instantly.

Emitting Stock Updates

On the server, you implement a WebSocket route under Axum and Tokio that broadcasts stock changes whenever an order is created. For example, in **src/server/ws.rs**:

```
use axum::{
    extract::ws::{WebSocketUpgrade, Message, WebSocket},
    response::IntoResponse,
};
use futures_util::{SinkExt, StreamExt};
use serde_json::json;
use crate::orders;
pub async fn stock_updates_ws(ws: WebSocketUpgrade) -> impl
IntoResponse {
    ws.on_upgrade(handle_socket)
}
async fn handle_socket(mut socket: WebSocket) {
    // In a real app, subscribe to a broadcast channel here
    while let Some(Ok(msg)) = socket.next().await {
        if let Message::Text(_) = msg {
            // ignore client pings
        }
```

```
    }
}
// When creating an order:
let update = json!({ "id": book_id, "stock": new_stock });
let _ = BROADCAST_CHANNEL.send(update.to_string());
```

We finally combine this with a broadcast channel so that each connected client receives updates. When you've got our reactive signal set up, a WebSocket feed pushing updates, and a server that notifies you of stock changes on order events, you'll see that our home page now stays in sync with inventory without needing to refresh the page. You can see real-time stock levels as you shop, which makes for a really interactive experience.

Summary

To sum up the learnings from this chapter, you very well added the WebAssembly support with accompanying JavaScript bindings. You modified our **index.html** to import and initialize the WebAssembly bundle, ensuring our UI mounted seamlessly in the browser. Next, you built a responsive home page in VS Code, wherein you learned to create a **HomePage** component that can fetch book data from our REST API and able to serve the static assets via a simple file server. You then learned to refactor UI elements into reusable Leptos components—**Card**, **Button**, and **SearchForm**—each accepting props and encapsulating styling, allowing you to replace inline markup with clean component usage.

Finally, you implemented client-state management using Leptos signals, storing our book list and updating it via both REST fetches and a WebSocket connection. You also have learned to write codes to open a WebSocket to **/ws/stock_updates**, parsing the incoming JSON into stock update objects, and mutating the **books** signal so that Leptos automatically re-render the affected cards.

CHAPTER 7: REAL-TIME INTERACTIONS USING WEBSOCKET

Overview

In this chapter, at the start, you will setup full-duplex WebSocket channels in our Axum server. We will be implementing an upgrade handler that registers incoming connections, subscribes them to the broadcast stream, and forwards JSON messages in real time. On the client side, we will write a Leptos component that opens a WebSocket connection, listens for message events, parses each payload into typed structures, and updates reactive signals so our UI reflects changes instantly.

Next, we will simulate live order status updates on the server by emitting "pending," "confirmed," and "shipped" events in a background Tokio task after an order is placed. We will also build an **`OrderTracker`** component that filters and displays these statuses as they arrive. To make sure everything works right, we will install Playwright, write tests that place orders via REST, go to the tracking page, and check that each status update appears within the right timeout. At last, we will expand our GitHub Actions workflow to launch the app, apply migrations, and run our Playwright suite on every pull request. This'll make sure that real-time functionality stays solid throughout development.

Implementing Websockets

We know that the websockets have become a cornerstone of real-time interaction. They provide a full-duplex communication channel over a single TCP connection, allowing servers to push data to clients as soon as events occur. Here, we will learn to set up a broadcast channel in our Axum server, and write client-side Leptos code that opens a WebSocket connection to receive live updates.

Our Axum server already includes Tokio and Tower HTTP, but to enable WebSocket support you must ensure our **`Cargo.toml`** enables the necessary features. In our **`[dependencies]`** section, verify you have:

```
axum = { version = "0.6", features = ["ws", "headers"] }
tokio = { version = "1", features = ["full"] }
futures-util = "0.3"
```

Establishing Broadcast Channel and WebSocket Endpoint

On the server, you create a global Tokio broadcast channel that any part of our application can use to send messages to all connected clients. In **`src/server/ws.rs`**, we then define and export the channel sender:

```
use tokio::sync::broadcast::{self, Sender};
```

```
use once_cell::sync::Lazy;
/// A global broadcast channel for sending JSON-encoded
updates.
pub static BROADCAST_SENDER: Lazy<Sender<String>> =
Lazy::new(|| {
    // Buffer size 16 for pending messages
    let (tx, _) = broadcast::channel(16);
    tx
});
```

Next, we then implement the WebSocket upgrade handler that registers each new connection to receive broadcast messages:

```
// src/server/ws.rs (continued)
use axum::{
    extract::ws::{WebSocketUpgrade, WebSocket, Message},
    response::IntoResponse,
    Router, routing::get,
};
use futures_util::{StreamExt, SinkExt};
/// Mount this route at "/ws/notifications"
pub fn ws_router() -> Router {
    Router::new().route("/ws/notifications", get(ws_handler))
}
async fn ws_handler(ws: WebSocketUpgrade) -> impl IntoResponse
{
    ws.on_upgrade(move |socket| handle_socket(socket))
}
async fn handle_socket(mut socket: WebSocket) {
    // Subscribe to the broadcast channel
    let mut rx = BROADCAST_SENDER.subscribe();
    // Loop: forward each broadcast message to the WebSocket
```

```
    while let Ok(msg) = rx.recv().await {
        if socket.send(Message::Text(msg)).await.is_err() {
            // Client disconnected
            break;
        }
    }
}
```

Within our **main.rs**, we then mount this router alongside our REST and GraphQL routes:

```
use crate::ws::ws_router;
// ...
let app = Router::new()
    // existing routes...
    .merge(ws_router())
    .layer(TraceLayer::new_for_http())
    .with_state(state.clone());
```

Now, whenever our application needs to push an update—such as after processing an order—you simply serialize the event to a JSON string and call:

```
let update = serde_json::json!({ "event": "order_placed",
"order_id": 42 });
let _ = BROADCAST_SENDER.send(update.to_string());
```

After this, all the connected clients will receive this message immediately.

Opening WebSocket in Leptos

On the frontend, we then use the WebAssembly's **web_sys** API to open a WebSocket connection and wire incoming messages into Leptos signals. To do this we addthe following in the **src/client/home_page.rs**:

```
use leptos::*;
use wasm_bindgen::JsCast;
use web_sys::MessageEvent;
```

```
use serde::Deserialize;
#[derive(Deserialize)]
struct Notification {
    event: String,
    order_id: i32,
}
#[component]
pub fn Notifications(cx: Scope) -> Element {
    let notifications = create_signal(cx,
Vec::<Notification>::new());
    // Establish WebSocket and handle incoming messages
    spawn_local(async move {
        let ws =
web_sys::WebSocket::new("ws://localhost:3000/ws/notifications"
)
            .expect("Failed to connect WebSocket");

        let notifications_clone = notifications.clone();
        let onmessage = Closure::wrap(Box::new(move |event:
MessageEvent| {
            if let Ok(text) = event.data().as_string() {
                if let Ok(note) =
serde_json::from_str::<Notification>(&text) {
                    notifications_clone.update(|list|
list.push(note));
                }
            }
        }) as Box<dyn FnMut(_)>);

ws.set_onmessage(Some(onmessage.as_ref().unchecked_ref()));
        onmessage.forget();
```

```
    });
    view! { cx,
        <div class="notifications">
            {for notifications.get().iter().map(|note| view! {
cx,
                <p>{format!("Event: {}, Order ID: {}",
note.event, note.order_id)}</p>
            })}
        </div>
    }
}
```

After this, include **<Notifications/>** in our **HomePage** to display real-time messages as they arrive.

Pushing Live Notifications and Updates

To see this in action, simply we shall start our server and open multiple browser tabs pointing at our home page. When a new order is created—either via REST or GraphQL—and our server calls **BROADCAST_SENDER.send(...)**, every connected client will instantly render the new notification.

Adding Dynamic Feedback Mechanisms

When you place an order in LibroCommerce, you expect more than just a confirmation page, rather you crave real-time insight into each step of our purchase. So here, we will try to enrich our app with live order tracking and instant notifications. We will see how, from the moment an order is created, status updates flow through our WebSocket channel and appear in the UI without a page reload.

Simulating Live Order Status Events

Let us consider that an order moving from "pending" to "confirmed" to "shipped" in just seconds. In our **create_order_handler**, you already broadcast the initial "pending" event. Now, you and I will add a small Tokio task that emits subsequent statuses after short delays.

Following is the quick revisesd script:

```
// after creating the order record...
```

```
let order_id = order.id;
// "pending" was sent earlier
tokio::spawn(async move {
    // Pause briefly, then push "confirmed"

tokio::time::sleep(tokio::time::Duration::from_secs(5)).await;
    let _ = BROADCAST_SENDER.send(
        serde_json::json!({ "order_id": order_id, "status":
"confirmed" }).to_string()
    );
    // Another pause, then "shipped"

tokio::time::sleep(tokio::time::Duration::from_secs(5)).await;
    let _ = BROADCAST_SENDER.send(
        serde_json::json!({ "order_id": order_id, "status":
"shipped" }).to_string()
    );
});
```

With these lines in place, every connected client will receive status messages spaced five seconds apart. We will see how easily a few lines of async code create a dynamic, time-based update stream.

Building an Interactive OrderTracker Component

The turning of server broadcasts into on-screen feedback happens only in the frontend. To do this, we add **order_tracker.rs** under **src/client/components**. In this component, we will listen on the same WebSocket channel and append statuses to a list as they arrive:

```
// src/client/components/order_tracker.rs
use leptos::*;
use wasm_bindgen::JsCast;
use web_sys::MessageEvent;
use serde::Deserialize;
#[derive(Deserialize, Clone)]
```

```
struct OrderEvent { order_id: i32, status: String }
#[component]
pub fn OrderTracker(cx: Scope, order_id: i32) -> Element {
    let statuses = create_signal(cx, Vec::<String>::new());
    spawn_local(async move {
        let ws =
web_sys::WebSocket::new("ws://localhost:3000/ws/notifications"
)
            .expect("WebSocket connection failed");
        let statuses_clone = statuses.clone();
        // Whenever a message arrives, parse and update
        let on_msg = Closure::wrap(Box::new(move |e:
MessageEvent| {
            if let Ok(txt) = e.data().as_string() {
                if let Ok(evt) =
serde_json::from_str::<OrderEvent>(&txt) {
                    if evt.order_id == order_id {
                        statuses_clone.update(|list|
list.push(evt.status.clone()));
                    }
                }
            }
        }) as Box<dyn FnMut(_)>);

ws.set_onmessage(Some(on_msg.as_ref().unchecked_ref()));
        on_msg.forget();
    });
    view! { cx,
        <div class="order-tracker">
            <h3>{format!("Tracking Order #{}", order_id)}</h3>
            <ul>
```

```
                {for statuses.get().iter().map(|s| view! { cx, <li>{s.clone()}</li> })}
            </ul>
        </div>
    }
}
```

Here, every time our server emits a status, this component captures it and pushes it into the **statuses** signal. The Leptos automatically re-renders the list, so you watch each step appear live.

With the server broadcasting and the **OrderTracker** in place, refresh our browser on the checkout confirmation page. Immediately after you submit an order, the "pending" will pop into view. Without touching the keyboard, "confirmed" follows five seconds later, then "shipped" five seconds after that. This real-time feedback creates a sense of connection between you, the app, and the underlying processes—exactly the kind of dynamic experience modern users expect.

End-to-end Testing of Real-time Flows

We will now set up an end-to-end test suite using Playwright, which drives a headless browser, simulates user actions, and asserts that our Leptos frontend displays the status updates pushed over WebSockets.

To begin with, we will first add Playwright to our project. In the root of the project, run the following:

```
npm init -y
npm install --save-dev @playwright/test
npx playwright install
```

This bootstraps a minimal Node environment, installs Playwright's test runner, and adds browser binaries. Next, add a test script to our **package.json**:

```
// package.json (snippet)
"scripts": {
  "test:e2e": "playwright test"
}
```

Create a new file at **e2e/order-status.spec.ts** and import Playwright's testing API.

We will launch our server (make sure it's running on **http://localhost:3000**), navigate to the confirmation page with a freshly placed order, then watch the UI update as statuses stream in.

Writing E2E Test

```
import { test, expect } from '@playwright/test';

test.describe('Real-Time Order Tracking', () => {

  let orderId: number;

  test.beforeAll(async () => {

    // Place a new order via REST so we know the orderId in
advance

    const response = await
fetch('http://localhost:3000/api/orders', {

      method: 'POST',

      headers: { 'Content-Type': 'application/json',
'Authorization': 'Bearer <token>' },

      body: JSON.stringify({

        user_id: 1,

        book_ids: [1],

        total: 9.99,

        card_token: 'test'

      })

    });

    const data = await response.json();

    orderId = data.id;

  });

  test(`should display order ${orderId} status updates`, async
({ page }) => {

    await
page.goto(`http://localhost:8080/orders/${orderId}`); // our
client route
```

```
    // Verify initial "pending" appears
    await expect(page.locator('li')).toContainText('pending');
    // Confirm "confirmed" shows up within 7 seconds
    await
expect(page.locator('li')).toContainText('confirmed', {
timeout: 7000 });
    // Finally, "shipped" appears within 12 seconds
    await expect(page.locator('li')).toContainText('shipped',
{ timeout: 12000 });
  });
});
```

In this test, **beforeAll** places an order through our REST endpoint and captures its ID. The test then loads the client route that includes the **<OrderTracker>** component for that ID. The Playwright's **expect** with timeouts ensures the UI reflects each server-sent status in the expected sequence.

Integrating E2E Tests into CI

Now to automate these checks on every pull request, we will extend our GitHub Actions workflow by adding the following in **.github/workflows/ci.yml**:

```
- name: Set up Node.js
  uses: actions/setup-node@v3
  with:
    node-version: '16'
- name: Install Playwright and run E2E tests
  run: |
    npm install
    npx playwright install --with-deps
    npm run test:e2e
```

After doing this, we need to ensure that our application server and a simple file server for WebAssembly assets are started in the background before the Playwright step. You can add a step that launches our Rust server via **cargo run &** and serves **static/** with a lightweight HTTP server, then waits briefly before running tests.

Summary

To conclude, we successfully enabled the WebSocket support in Axum by selecting the **`ws`** feature and adding **`futures-util`**. We then created a global Tokio broadcast channel to fan out JSON-encoded messages. You implemented a WebSocket upgrade handler at **`/ws/notifications`** that subscribes each connection to the channel and forwards every broadcasted message.

On the frontend, you opened a WebSocket in a Leptos component, attached a **`MessageEvent`** listener, parsed incoming JSON into strongly typed events, and updated a Leptos signal so the UI re-rendered automatically. To add dynamic feedback, you enhanced the **`create_order_handler`** to spawn a background task that emitted "pending," "confirmed," and "shipped" status updates with timed delays, leveraging the same broadcast channel. You then built an **`OrderTracker`** component that takes an **`order_id`** prop, listens for matching events, and pushes each new status into its signal-backed list. For full confidence, you set up end-to-end tests using Playwright: a headless browser test placed an order via REST, navigated to the order page, and asserted that each status appeared in sequence within defined timeouts.

Finally, you integrated these tests into our GitHub Actions pipeline, spinning up the server and static assets, running migrations, and executing Playwright checks on every push. All these practical steps ensured that LibroCommerce's real-time interactions work seamlessly from server to browser under continuous validation.

CHAPTER 8: MODERN SECURITY, PERFORMANCE, AND CLOUD STRATEGIES

Overview

First, we'll secure every connection with TLS termination via Rustls, so all traffic runs over HTTPS. You can reinforce this by adding HSTS and a strict Content Security Policy so browsers refuse to downgrade or load untrusted resources. Next, we will use **Redis** and **HttpOnly** cookies to manage sessions on the server-side, which'll let you revoke sessions right away and protect user data. Once you've secured our system, we will adjust our asynchronous runtime by tweaking Tokio's thread pool and fine-tuning the sqlx connection pool parameters. This'll help you handle a lot of activity without any delays. We will learn how to stream large result sets directly to clients to reduce memory pressure and apply client-side techniques—like debouncing user inputs and limiting concurrent tasks—to keep our frontend responsive under heavy load.

Then, we will package each microservice and the WebAssembly-based frontend into Docker images using multi-stage builds. After that, we will deploy them with Kubernetes, leveraging deployments, services, and rolling updates for zero-downtime releases. At last, we will set up our app and host system with real-time monitoring. This means we will create perf-monitor-rs collectors for CPU and memory metrics, add application-level counters and histograms around our HTTP handlers, and expose a Prometheus endpoint. Once you've got all that data in Grafana, you can set up dashboards and alerts to keep an eye on performance and reliability. That'll give you a full picture of how to build, secure, and run a modern web app at scale.

Encrypting and Securing App

Well! First let me tell you that we have built a feature-rich backend and a dynamic front end. Now it's time to lock everything down. Let's think about the experience of our users. First, they have to log in, then place orders, and look at sensitive data—and all of that happens over insecure channels. We'll keep it secure by making sure HTTPS is used everywhere, telling browsers to only use TLS, adding strict security headers, and managing sessions with HttpOnly cookies that are supported by Redis. Let's dive in together.

Terminating HTTPS with Rustls

By now our server's core router lives in **create_app()**. To wrap that in TLS, you only need to point Axum-Server at our PEM files. In our **main.rs**, we then replace the plain **bind** call with this snippet:

```
// Load our certs once at startup
let cert_chain =
tokio::fs::read("certs/fullchain.pem").await.unwrap();
let private_key =
tokio::fs::read("certs/privkey.pem").await.unwrap();
```

```
let tls_config =
axum_server::tls_rustls::RustlsConfig::from_pem(cert_chain,
private_key)
    .await
    .unwrap();
// Serve our app over HTTPS
axum_server::bind("0.0.0.0:443")
    .tls_config(tls_config)
    .serve(create_app().await.into_make_service())
    .await
    .unwrap();
```

With this in place, every connection is encrypted. If you peek at our browser's network tab, we will see only **https://** requests—and no more red warnings.

Enforcing Browser Security with Headers

Even on HTTPS, you can harden our app by telling browsers, "Only talk TLS," and "Only load scripts I trust." Just insert a middleware layer that adds HSTS and CSP headers right before our routes:

```
async fn security_headers<B>(req: Request<B>, next: Next<B>) -
> Response {
    let mut response = next.run(req).await;
    let headers = response.headers_mut();
    headers.insert(
        header::STRICT_TRANSPORT_SECURITY,
        "max-age=63072000; includeSubDomains;
preload".parse().unwrap()
    );
    headers.insert(
        header::CONTENT_SECURITY_POLICY,
        "default-src 'self'; script-src 'self'; style-src
'self'".parse().unwrap()
    );
```

```
    response
}
// In our router setup:
Router::new()
    // ... our routes ...
    .layer(from_fn(security_headers))
    .with_state(state)
```

Now browsers will refuse to downgrade to HTTP and only execute scripts and styles served from our domain.

Robust Session Management with Redis

Next, rather than stuffing user state into JWTs, we will keep sessions server-side for instant revocation. Our Redis store and session layer were wired up earlier; here's how you read and write session data in a handler:

```
async fn login_handler(
    ReadableSession(session): ReadableSession,
    mut WritableSession(mut session): WritableSession,
    Json(credentials): Json<LoginPayload>,
) -> impl IntoResponse {
    // After validating credentials...
    session.insert("user_id", user.id).unwrap();
    (StatusCode::OK, "Logged in successfully")
}
async fn profile_handler(
    ReadableSession(session): ReadableSession
) -> impl IntoResponse {
    if let Some(user_id) = session.get::<i32>("user_id") {
        let profile = fetch_user_profile(user_id).await;
        Json(profile)
    } else {
```

```
        (StatusCode::UNAUTHORIZED, "Please log in")
    }
}
async fn logout_handler(
    mut session: WritableSession
) -> impl IntoResponse {
    session.destroy();
    (StatusCode::OK, "Logged out")
}
```

Because the cookie is marked **Secure** and **HttpOnly** by default, no JavaScript can steal it—and you can call **destroy()** to revoke access immediately when a user logs out.

Just to conlclude, by getting our entire server in TLS, layering on HSTS and a tight CSP, and handling sessions in Redis with protected cookies, we were able to transform our app into a fortress without sacrificing performance or developer ergonomics. The users can now browse, log in, and place orders with confidence that their data is always encrypted and their sessions under our control.

Asynchronous Processing and Tuning

When traffic surges and tons of users hit LibroCommerce at once, you expect every request to be handled quickly, without any blocking or lag. Here, we're going to tweak the server and client to handle a lot of activity at once. We'll adjust our Tokio runtime, optimize the SQLX connection pool, and stream large datasets efficiently. We'll also apply client-side debouncing and resource loading to keep our app responsive under load.

Leveraging Tokio's Runtime

By default, our **#[tokio::main]** macro spins up a multi-threaded executor sized to our CPU cores. To squeeze out more performance under heavy load, you can customize the number of worker threads and the max blocking threads.

So here, within our **main.rs**, we replace with an explicit runtime builder:

```
#[tokio::main]
async fn main() {
    // ...
```

```
}
use tokio::runtime::Builder;
fn main() {
    let runtime = Builder::new_multi_thread()
        .worker_threads(8)                  // increase if you
have many cores
        .max_blocking_threads(16)           // for blocking
operations
        .enable_all()
        .build()
        .unwrap();
    runtime.block_on(async {
        // initialize .env, tracing, and state
        let app = create_app().await;
        axum_server::bind("0.0.0.0:443")
            .serve(app.into_make_service())
            .await
            .unwrap();
    });
}
```

With this, our server can schedule thousands of async tasks across a tuned thread pool. You might experiment with **`worker_threads`** slightly above our CPU count if you expect many I/O-bound tasks.

Tuning SQLx Connection Pool

We know that our **`PgPool`** is the gateway to PostgreSQL, and so under peak load, there is a possibility that the connections can exhaust or queue. So here, we can adjust the pool settings in **`db.rs`**:

```
use sqlx::postgres::PgPoolOptions;
pub async fn init_db_pool() -> PgPool {
    let database_url = std::env::var("DATABASE_URL").unwrap();
```

```
    PgPoolOptions::new()
        .max_connections(20)            // higher than
default 10
        .min_connections(5)             // keep some ready
        .connect_timeout(std::time::Duration::from_secs(5))
        .acquire_timeout(std::time::Duration::from_secs(2))
        .idle_timeout(std::time::Duration::from_secs(300))
        .connect(&database_url)
        .await
        .unwrap()
}
```

In the above, we raised the **max_connections**, and it will let us more concurrent queries, while **acquire_timeout** ensures requests don't hang indefinitely.

Streaming Large Data Sets Efficiently

For endpoints returning thousands of records—such as a full order history—you avoid buffering everything into memory by streaming rows. And to do this, we replace **fetch_all** with a row stream in our handler:

```
use axum::body::StreamBody;
use futures_util::stream::TryStreamExt;
async fn stream_orders(
    State(state): State<AppState>
) -> impl IntoResponse {
    let stream = sqlx::query_as!(
        Order,
        "SELECT id, user_id, book_ids, total, transaction_id
FROM orders"
    )
    .fetch(&state.db_pool)
    .map_ok(|order| {
        serde_json::to_string(&order).unwrap() + "\n"
```

```
    });
    let body = StreamBody::new(stream);
    Response::builder()
        .header(CONTENT_TYPE, "application/json")
        .body(body)
        .unwrap()
}
```

This code sends each order as a newline-delimited JSON object, allowing clients to process the stream incrementally and reducing server memory pressure.

Client-Side Async Patterns and Debouncing

On the frontend, rapid user interactions—like typing in a search box—can trigger excessive network calls. So here what we can do is, we can debounce input events so that you only fetch new results after the user pauses briefly:

```
// In SearchForm or HomePage component
let search_term = create_signal(cx, "".to_string());
let debounced = create_debounced_signal(cx,
search_term.clone(), Duration::from_millis(300));
spawn_local(async move {
    debounced.with_listener(move |term| {
        spawn_local(async move {
            let results: Vec<Book> =
reqwest::get(&format!("/api/books/search?query={}", term))
                .await.unwrap()
                .json().await.unwrap();
            // update our books signal
        });
    });
});
```

Here, the **create_debounced_signal** ensures the handler only runs once 300 ms have passed without further input, cutting network chatter.

Backpressure and Task Limiting

Sometimes, you want to limit concurrent tasks—for instance, when prefetching data on scroll events. A simple semaphore does the trick:

```
use tokio::sync::Semaphore;

let semaphore = Arc::new(Semaphore::new(5)); // only 5
concurrent tasks

spawn_local({

    let sem = semaphore.clone();

    async move {

        let permit = sem.acquire().await.unwrap();

        // fetch data...

        drop(permit); // release for next task

    }

});
```

This pattern prevents our app from launching dozens of inflight requests that could swamp the server or the client's own resources.

By calibrating our Tokyo runtime, optimizing connection pools, streaming data instead of buffering, debouncing client-side events, and applying backpressure controls, you can outfit LibroCommerce to handle high traffic smoothly. Even if you've got ten users or ten thousand, our app will stay responsive, efficient, and ready for any size deployment.

Containerization and Orchestration

Nowadays, microservices need to run in their own isolated, reproducible environment, and Kubernetes is the go-to way to manage those containers when they're out there in force. I'll show you how packaging our Rust microservices and frontend into Docker images simplifies deployment, and how Kubernetes helps you deploy, scale, and roll out updates across a cluster.

Embracing Containers and Kubernetes

Basically, the containers let you combine our application code, its runtime, and all its dependencies into one package. There's no more "it worked on my machine" mystery—every environment, from our laptop to production, runs the same image. Platforms like Kubernetes then take those images and handle scheduling, health checks, self-healing, and zero-downtime updates automatically. Rather than manually SSHing into servers, you just declare the desired state—like three replicas of our inventory service—and Kubernetes takes care of the rest.

Writing Multi-Stage Dockerfile

We begin with, at first packaging the **`inventory`** service by simply creating the **`inventory/Dockerfile`** as below:

```
# Stage 1: Build
FROM rust:1.65 as builder
WORKDIR /usr/src/inventory
COPY inventory/Cargo.toml inventory/Cargo.lock ./
RUN mkdir src && echo "fn main(){}" > src/main.rs
RUN cargo build --release
COPY inventory/ ./
RUN rm src/main.rs
RUN cargo build --release
# Stage 2: Minimal Runtime
FROM debian:buster-slim
WORKDIR /app
# Install only needed libs (if any), then copy the binary
COPY --from=builder
/usr/src/inventory/target/release/inventory .
CMD ["./inventory"]
```

We then switch to the **`inventory`** folder and build the image:

```
docker build -t librocommerce/inventory:latest .
```

Same as above, we have to then repeat the same pattern for **`orders/`** and **`user_accounts/`**.

Containerizing Frontend

As for our Leptos-WebAssembly frontend, just use a basic Nginx image. Go ahead and create something like **`frontend/Dockerfile`**:

```
FROM node:16 as builder
WORKDIR /usr/src/app
COPY static/package.json static/package-lock.json ./
RUN npm install
COPY static/ ./
RUN npm run build   # if you have a build step
FROM nginx:stable-alpine
COPY --from=builder /usr/src/app/dist /usr/share/nginx/html
```

Then build and tag the following:

```
docker build -t librocommerce/frontend:latest -f
frontend/Dockerfile .
```

After this, simply push each of the images to our container registry:

```
docker tag librocommerce/inventory:latest
registry.example.com/librocommerce/inventory:latest
docker push
registry.example.com/librocommerce/inventory:latest
# Repeat for orders, user_accounts, frontend
```

Defining Kubernetes Manifests

Now that the images are in our registry, we can go ahead to declare how they run in Kubernetes.for which we access the **k8s/inventory-deployment.yaml** and edit it as shown below:

```
apiVersion: apps/v1
kind: Deployment
metadata:
  name: inventory
spec:
  replicas: 3
  selector:
    matchLabels:
```

```yaml
      app: inventory
  template:
    metadata:
      labels:
        app: inventory
    spec:
      containers:
      - name: inventory
        image:
registry.example.com/librocommerce/inventory:latest
        ports:
        - containerPort: 3000
---
apiVersion: v1
kind: Service
metadata:
  name: inventory
spec:
  type: ClusterIP
  selector:
    app: inventory
  ports:
  - port: 80
    targetPort: 3000
```

We then create similar **orders-deployment.yaml**, **user-accounts-deployment.yaml**, and a **frontend-deployment.yaml** pointing to the Nginx container on port 80, exposed via a LoadBalancer Service for external access.

Deploying and Managing with kubectl

Then we just apply all the manifests from our project root:

```
kubectl apply -f k8s/
```

Then we shall check the rollout status:

```
kubectl rollout status deployment/inventory
kubectl get pods
```

Simply try to scale a service:

```
kubectl scale deployment/inventory --replicas=5
```

And do not forget to update the image version in our Deployment manifest. Or you can simply use the following snippet:

```
kubectl set image deployment/inventory
inventory=registry.example.com/librocommerce/inventory:v2
```

The Kubernetes will then finally perform a zero-downtime rolling update.

Therefore, by keeping each microservice and the frontend in their own Docker image and using Kubernetes to deploy them, you end up with a scalable, resilient infrastructure.

Real-Time Monitoring

Now, when you're rolling out an app on a large scale, you need more than just logs. You need to be able to see how your system's doing in real time. We need to set up monitoring in our app by combining a system-level profiler with application-level metrics. To do this, we'll use **perf-monitor-rs** to track CPU and memory usage, and the **metrics** ecosystem to keep track of request counts and latencies. If we expose a Prometheus endpoint, we'll be able to scrape these metrics in real time and visualize them in tools like Grafana to get us the insights we need to troubleshoot and optimize under load.

Capturing System Metrics

So here, we begin with setting up the **perf-monitor-rs** to sample the CPU and memory usage periodically. So here, in our **main.rs**, we spawn a background task just after initializing our Tokio runtime:

```
use perf_monitor_rs::{PerfMonitor, Resource};
use metrics::{gauge, Unit};
use std::time::Duration;
```

```
async fn spawn_system_monitor() {
    let mut monitor = PerfMonitor::new().unwrap();
    // Select CPU and memory sampling at 5-second intervals
    monitor.add_resource(Resource::Cpu).unwrap();
    monitor.add_resource(Resource::Memory).unwrap();
    monitor.start(Duration::from_secs(5), move |data| {
        // Record gauges for each metric
        gauge!("system_cpu_usage", data.cpu_usage_percent(),
Unit::Percent);
        gauge!("system_memory_usage",
data.memory_usage_bytes(), Unit::Bytes);
    });
}
#[tokio::main]
async fn main() {
    // ... load env, tracing, state, etc.
    tokio::spawn(spawn_system_monitor());
    let app = create_app().await;
    // ... bind and serve
}
```

As per the above snippet, every five seconds our application will collect the host's CPU percentage and memory usage, and then records them as gauges. We will see exactly how the system behaves when it is etiher put under stress or going through a heavy traffic.

Instrumenting HTTP Handlers with App Metrics

Next, we will then add counters and histograms around our REST and GraphQL handlers so you can track traffic and latency. So here, in **handlers.rs**, we will then import the metrics macros and wrap our existing code:

```
use metrics::{increment_counter, histogram};
use std::time::Instant;
#[instrument(skip_all)]
```

```
pub async fn list_books_handler(
    State(state): State<AppState>
) -> Json<Vec<Book>> {
    let start = Instant::now();
    let rows = sqlx::query_as!(Book, /* ... */)
        .fetch_all(&state.db_pool)
        .await
        .unwrap_or_default();
    increment_counter!("http_requests_total", "method" =>
"GET", "endpoint" => "/api/books");
    histogram!("http_request_duration_seconds",
start.elapsed().as_secs_f64(), "endpoint" => "/api/books");
    Json(rows)
}
```

Now here, each time the handler runs, you log an incremented counter and record how long the operation took. We need to repeat this pattern in our other core handlers in order to achieve the full coverage.

Exposing Prometheus-scrapable Endpoint

With metrics flowing, you need to serve them to a monitoring system. So here, we add a handler in **src/server/metrics.rs**:

```
use async_trait::async_trait;
use axum::{response::IntoResponse, http::StatusCode};
use metrics_exporter_prometheus::{PrometheusBuilder,
PrometheusHandle};
pub fn init_metrics() -> PrometheusHandle {
    PrometheusBuilder::new()
        .install_recorder()
        .unwrap()
}
```

```
pub async fn metrics_handler(handle: PrometheusHandle) -> impl
IntoResponse {
    let body = handle.render();
    (StatusCode::OK, [("Content-Type", "text/plain;
version=0.0.4")], body)
}
```

And in **main.rs**, we then initialize and mount it:

```
let prom_handle = init_metrics();
let app = Router::new()
    // ... our existing routes ...
    .route("/metrics", get(move ||
metrics_handler(prom_handle.clone())))
    .with_state(state);
```

Now here, we can witness that the Prometheus can hit **/metrics** to pull both our system and application metrics in a single unified stream.

There's more to consider, like system-level sampling, application-level counters, and a Prometheus endpoint. With these, you can transform LibroCommerce into a fully observable platform. No matter what kind of load you've got going on, we've got the real-time data you need to figure out what's slowing things down, scale up your services, and keep things running smoothly for your users.

Summary

To sum it up, you figured out how to set up our Axum server to use Rustls for TLS and added HSTS and CSP headers to boost browser security. You used a Redis-backed session store with HttpOnly cookies to manage user sessions securely and revoke them on demand. To handle the high traffic, you customized Tokio's runtime with more worker and blocking threads, tuned our SQLX pool for optimal connections, and refactored large data endpoints to stream results incrementally. On the client side, you put in place debounced signals and semaphores to control the rate of requests and keep the user interface responsive.

Then, you put each Rust microservice and the Leptos front end into multi-stage Docker images and deployed them with Kubernetes. You also defined deployments, services, and zero-downtime rolling updates. You brought in real-time observability by creating perf-monitor-rs tasks to record system metrics and putting metrics counters and histograms into HTTP handlers. All of this was served at a Prometheus-scrapable **/metrics** endpoint. We will also set up Grafana dashboards and alerts to visualize CPU, memory, and request-latency trends. By doing all this, our production environment remains transparent and that any performance degradation is detected and addressed immediately.

Chapter 9: Cloud-native Releases and Continuous Delivery

Overview

In this chapter you will orchestrate truly hands-off delivery of LibroCommerce. You will start by leveraging the Docker images you previously created, defining Kubernetes manifests to run each service in Deployments and exposing them via Services. You will write a GitHub Actions workflow that triggers on pull requests and merges to **main**, automatically running Rust unit and integration tests, Playwright end-to-end checks, and then building, tagging, and pushing our container images only after tests pass. Next, you will configure the same workflow to deploy updates to our Kubernetes cluster with zero-downtime rolling updates, using **kubectl set image** and monitoring rollout status, while sending alerts on failures.

After mastering continuous delivery, you will explore how to move latency-sensitive and spiky workloads into serverless functions with AWS Lambda using AWS SAM, paying only for actual execution time and scaling to zero. You will then deploy our Leptos server-side rendering logic to a global edge network via Cloudflare Workers, dramatically reducing Time to First Byte for users worldwide. By combining orchestrated containers, serverless functions, and edge compute, you will achieve an automated, resilient, and high-performance release pipeline that requires no manual steps—from code commit to production serving.

Leveraging Docker Images

You've already built and pushed Docker images for each service and our frontend. Now the situation is that for every new release—say **v1.2.0**—our CI system automatically builds fresh images, pushes them to our registry, and rolls them out to our Kubernetes cluster with zero downtime. This may become a repetitive job for our developers and so, I was thinking if we set up a GitHub Actions workflow that watches for version tags, rebuilds and pushes our images, then updates each Deployment in Kubernetes, then it will be an ease for our development team in handling rollouts and the automatic rollbacks on failure.

So, let us try out in the following:

Triggering on Semantic Version Tags

We don't want our pipeline to run until you've polished a release. By using Git tags like **v1.2.0**, you ensure **main** remains free for work in progress. In **.github/workflows/cd.yml**, we start with:

```
name: Continuous Delivery
on:
  push:
    tags:
```

```
      - 'v*.*.*'   # any tag matching vMAJOR.MINOR.PATCH
```

As soon as you run **`git tag v1.2.0 && git push --tags`**, this workflow kicks off.

Building and Pushing Docker Images

Now here, the first job builds images for each microservice and the frontend, tags them with the Git tag, and pushes them to our registry:

```
jobs:
  build_and_push:
    runs-on: ubuntu-latest
    outputs:
      tag: ${{ github.ref_name }}
    steps:
      - uses: actions/checkout@v2
      - name: Set up Docker Buildx
        uses: docker/setup-buildx-action@v2
      - name: Log in to Registry
        uses: docker/login-action@v2
        with:
          registry: registry.example.com
          username: ${{ secrets.REGISTRY_USER }}
          password: ${{ secrets.REGISTRY_PASS }}
      - name: Build & Push Inventory Service
        uses: docker/build-push-action@v3
        with:
          context: ./inventory
          file: ./inventory/Dockerfile
          push: true
          tags:
registry.example.com/librocommerce/inventory:${{
steps.tag.outputs.tag }}
```

```
      - name: Build & Push Orders Service
        uses: docker/build-push-action@v3
        with:
          context: ./orders
          file: ./orders/Dockerfile
          push: true
          tags: registry.example.com/librocommerce/orders:${{
steps.tag.outputs.tag }}
      - name: Build & Push Frontend
        uses: docker/build-push-action@v3
        with:
          context: ./frontend
          file: ./frontend/Dockerfile
          push: true
          tags:
registry.example.com/librocommerce/frontend:${{
steps.tag.outputs.tag }}
```

After referencing **`${{ steps.tag.outputs.tag }}`** as shown in the above snippet, each image is versioned exactly to our Git tag.

Deploying to Kubernetes with Zero-Downtime

Once images are in the registry, the next job updates our cluster. It pulls the kubeconfig from a secret and uses **`kubectl set image`** to trigger rolling updates:

```
 deploy:
    needs: build_and_push
    runs-on: ubuntu-latest
    steps:
      - name: Download kubeconfig
        run: echo "${{ secrets.KUBE_CONFIG }}" > kubeconfig
      - name: Set up kubectl
        uses: azure/setup-kubectl@v3
```

```
        with:
          version: 'latest'
          kubeconfig: kubeconfig
      - name: Update Inventory Deployment
        run: |
          kubectl set image deployment/inventory \

inventory=registry.example.com/librocommerce/inventory:${{
needs.build_and_push.outputs.tag }} \
            --record
          kubectl rollout status deployment/inventory
      - name: Update Orders Deployment
        run: |
          kubectl set image deployment/orders \

orders=registry.example.com/librocommerce/orders:${{
needs.build_and_push.outputs.tag }} \
            --record
          kubectl rollout status deployment/orders
      - name: Update Frontend Deployment
        run: |
          kubectl set image deployment/frontend \

frontend=registry.example.com/librocommerce/frontend:${{
needs.build_and_push.outputs.tag }} \
            --record
          kubectl rollout status deployment/frontend
```

Here, each **`rollout status`** ensures Kubernetes finishes the update gracefully before moving on.

Managing Rollbacks and Notifications

Coming to Kubernetes, it auto-reverts a Deployment if its new Pods fail health checks. To surface the failures in our CI, set the **--record** flag so you can inspect revision history. You can also add a final step to notify our team via Slack or email if any rollout fails:

```
      - name: Notify on Failure
        if: failure ()
        uses: some/slack-notify-action@v1
        with:
          webhook-url: ${{secrets. SLACK_WEBHOOK}}
          message: "! Deployment of tag
${{needs.build_and_push.outputs.tag}} failed."
```

With this CD pipeline in place, releasing a new version is as simple as tagging our repo. The GitHub Actions rebuilds containers, pushes them, and orchestrates rolling updates across our cluster with zero downtime and automatic rollbacks.

Configuring CI/CD Pipelines

Now here we are considering that we should have a system wherein we are never required to click "deploy" repeatedly. You've written tests, built Docker images, and defined our Kubernetes manifests—all that remains is wiring these pieces together so every code change flows from commit to production automatically. So here, we'll author a single GitHub Actions workflow that runs our unit and integration tests, builds and pushes Docker images, and rolls out updates to our cluster—all without manual steps.

Defining Workflow Trigger

To begin with, You and I will start creating an yml file called as **.github/workflows/ci-cd.yml**. We want tests to run on every pull request and pushes to **main**, but only deploy when code lands on **main**. So in our new workflow file, we then declare:

```
name: CI/CD Pipeline
on:
  pull_request:
    branches: [ main ]
  push:
    branches: [ main ]
```

After this, the contributors get immediate feedback when they open a PR, and merges into **main** kick off both testing and deployment.

Running Tests and Linting Automatically

Our first job, **tests**, uses Rust's toolchain and Playwright for E2E checks. It will install dependencies, spin up PostgreSQL, apply migrations, start the server, then execute both **cargo test** and our Playwright suite:

```
jobs:
  tests:
    runs-on: ubuntu-latest
    services:
      postgres:
        image: postgres:13
        env:
          POSTGRES_USER: libro_user
          POSTGRES_PASSWORD: secret
          POSTGRES_DB: libro_commerce
        ports:
          - 5432:5432
        options: >-
          --health-cmd "pg_isready -U libro_user"
          --health-interval 10s
          --health-timeout 5s
          --health-retries 5
    steps:
      - uses: actions/checkout@v2
      - name: Install Rust
        uses: actions-rs/toolchain@v1
        with:
          toolchain: stable
```

```
          override: true
      - name: Run Database Migrations
        run: diesel migration run
      - name: Run Rust Tests
        run: cargo test -- --test-threads=1
      - name: Set up Node.js for E2E
        uses: actions/setup-node@v3
        with:
          node-version: '16'
      - name: Install and Run Playwright
        run: |
          npm ci
          npx playwright install --with-deps
          npm run test:e2e
```

Here, every push or PR triggers this job. A failure here blocks merges and deployments, giving you confidence in every change.

Building, Tagging, and Pushing Docker Images

Once all the tests pass on a push to **`main`**, the **`build-and-push`** job takes over. It uses the Git tag or the **`main`** SHA as the image tag, building each microservice and the frontend, and pushing them to our registry:

```
  build-and-push:
    needs: tests
    runs-on: ubuntu-latest
    environment: production
    steps:
      - uses: actions/checkout@v2
      - name: Set up Docker Buildx
        uses: docker/setup-buildx-action@v2
      - name: Log in to Registry
```

```
        uses: docker/login-action@v2
        with:
          registry: registry.example.com
          username: ${{ secrets.REGISTRY_USER }}
          password: ${{ secrets.REGISTRY_PASS }}
      - name: Build & Push Services and Frontend
        uses: docker/build-push-action@v3
        with:
          context: .
          file: ./inventory/Dockerfile
          push: true
          tags: |

registry.example.com/librocommerce/inventory:latest
            registry.example.com/librocommerce/inventory:${{
github.sha }}
          cache-from:
type=registry,ref=registry.example.com/librocommerce/inventory
:latest
      # Repeat build-push-action for orders, user_accounts,
and frontend
```

By chaining on **`needs: tests`**, images are only built once code integrity is confirmed.

Automated Deployment to Kubernetes

With images in the registry, the final job **`deploy`** connects to our cluster and updates each Deployment. Using the same Git SHA tag ensures traceability:

```
 deploy:
    needs: build-and-push
    runs-on: ubuntu-latest
    if: github.ref == 'refs/heads/main'
    steps:
```

```
      - name: Configure kubectl
        uses: azure/setup-kubectl@v3
        with:
          version: 'latest'
          kubeconfig: ${{ secrets.KUBE_CONFIG }}
      - name: Deploy Inventory
        run: |
          kubectl set image deployment/inventory \

inventory=registry.example.com/librocommerce/inventory:${{
github.sha }} \
            --record
          kubectl rollout status deployment/inventory
      - name: Deploy Orders
        run: |
          kubectl set image deployment/orders \

orders=registry.example.com/librocommerce/orders:${{
github.sha }} \
            --record
          kubectl rollout status deployment/orders
      - name: Deploy Frontend
        run: |
          kubectl set image deployment/frontend \

frontend=registry.example.com/librocommerce/frontend:${{
github.sha }} \
            --record
          kubectl rollout status deployment/frontend
```

Because this job only runs on pushes to **`main`**, every change merged there automatically propagates to production, eliminating manual steps.

Zero Downtime and Safe Rollbacks

Now here, we are aware that the Kubernetes handles rolling updates by default—maintaining old Pods until new ones pass health checks. What should we do if something go wrong? although **kubectl rollout undo deployment/inventory** can revert instantly. So to bake this solution into our flow, we needt to expand the workflow as below:

```
      - name: Notify on Failure
        if: failure()
        uses: some/slack-notify-action@v1
        with:
          webhook-url: ${{ secrets.SLACK_WEBHOOK }}
          message: "Deployment failed at commit ${{ github.sha
}}"
```

Here, the alerts ensure you know immediately if a rollout misbehaves.

So, if we put all things together, we could say that we were able to construct a pipeline that, on every pull request, tests our code in full; and on every merge to **main**, rebuilds containers, pushes to our registry, and orchestrates a cluster-wide update with zero human clicks.

Summary

So, you got each Rust microservice and the WebAssembly frontend into multi-stage Docker images and pushed them to our container registry. Then you declared Kubernetes Deployments and Services for each component, applied them with kubectl apply, and performed zero-downtime rolling updates by setting new image tags. You saw how Kubernetes automatically handles scaling, self-healing, and rollbacks.

Then, you explored serverless and edge strategies. You moved the order-processing logic into AWS Lambda functions defined in an AWS SAM template, enabling on-demand scaling to zero. You also deployed our Leptos SSR bundle as a Cloudflare Worker to pre-render catalog pages at the network edge. By the time it was over, you had turned LibroCommerce into a fully cloud-native app that delivers performance, resilience, and continuous delivery with no manual interventions.

Index

A

B

C

D

E

G

H

I

J

K

L

M

N

Epilogue

Thinking about the journey we've been on through, gets me excited for what's coming in your work. At the start, you installed Rust, Leptos, and the tools that let you compile to WebAssembly. Then, you designed a service-oriented architecture that split your app into modules. Axum and Tokio were a piece of cake for you, and you nailed SQLx for asynchronous database access. You also crafted Serde models that flow seamlessly between client and server. Your endpoints were secured with JWT, OAuth2, Argon2 hashing, and TLS, and performance was tuned with custom Tokio runtimes, connection-pool tweaks, and streaming large datasets. With WebSockets, you've given your users instant feedback, tested real-time flows with Playwright, and automated every step in a CI/CD pipeline that builds, tests, containers, and deploys on every commit. And you even took your logic to the next level with serverless functions and edge workers, cutting down on latency and expanding globally without any manual intervention.

Now, you've got all these building blocks at your fingertips. Whether you need to solve a new challenge, spin up a Leptos component in the browser, or craft another microservice and deploy it in minutes, Rust crates have you covered. It's clear that you know how to validate performance metrics, roll back a failed rollout, and rewrite your code for an edge-first experience. Most importantly, you've seen how one language—Rust—can unify every layer of your stack, from low-level WebAssembly modules that run in the browser to high-throughput backends that power thousands of users.

Now it's time to take that first bold step beyond these examples. You can experiment with new crates, connect to different data stores, build custom WebAssembly plugins, or explore novel edge computing scenarios. Share your modules with the community, contribute to Leptos, or adapt these patterns to totally different domains—real-time games, collaborative editors, or data-intensive dashboards.

Thank You

www.ingramcontent.com/pod-product-compliance
Lightning Source LLC
Chambersburg PA
CBHW080214170726
48282CB00030B/1115
* 9 7 8 9 3 4 9 1 7 4 8 7 0 *